Who are You?

Gunas in R.K. Narayan's Men Protagonists

Who are You?

Gunas in R.K. Narayan's Men Protagonists

Roopa Shankar

KALPAZ

Revised, Updated Edition 2022

Published by

Kalpaz Publications
C-30, Satyawati Nagar,
Delhi – 110052
E-mail: kalpaz@hotmail.com
Ph.: 9212142040

Printed at: Gyan Press, Delhi

Cataloging in Publication Data—DK
Courtesy: D.K. Agencies (P) Ltd. <docinfo@dkagencies.com>

Shankar, Roopa, author.
Who are you? : R.K. Narayan's men protagonists under the dynamics of gunas / Roopa Shankar.
pages cm
ISBN 9789353243005

1. Narayan, R. K., 1906-2001—Characters—Men. 2. Characters and characteristics in literature. I. Title.

PR9499.3.N3Z87 2016 DDC 823.914 23

Contents

Contents

Acknowledgment

My deepest gratitude goes out to the brilliant writer *RK Narayan*. The wit, humour and wisdom he has incorporated in his novels, has made the journey of research immensely enjoyable.

Dr Rita Garg, Head of the Department of English, Ismail PG College, Meerut suggested this novel topic. First of its kind, it creatively amalgamates *RK Narayan's novels* with *Three modes of Nature (Gunas)*. Thank you, ma'am, for your constant support. Your supervision coupled with your inputs makes me proud of this work.

I extend my gratitude to *Dr Charu Gupta*, Professor, University of Delhi, for inspiring me, helping me with this study and giving me her unequivocal support. I have always looked up to her and continue to do so.

My mother, *Dr JL Majumdar*, a Sanskrit lecturer for thirty-three years of her life, is the reason I undertook this study. She has made me believe that pursuit of knowledge is beyond any boundaries. Thus, I decided to be a student, yet again at forty-four years, combining areas in Psychology, Sanskrit and English Literature respectively, for this research.

I bow my head in thanks to *Dr S Anandalakshmy,* my professor at Lady Irwin College, way back in 1986-1991. She ignited in me the spark of learning in formative college years. I feel the presence of Almighty in her. She is not physically among us anymore. However, she saw the first edition of this book. I love her. My gratitude and emotions for her, extend beyond the definition of words.

To my dear ma-in-law, *Shail Bala,* for encouraging me and constantly supporting my decisions pertaining to books and learning. I miss you.

I acknowledge the suggestion of *Professor Smita Agarwal*, Department of English, Central University of Allahabad. This aided me to make apt changes in the title of the book. I will remain immensely grateful.

Thank you, *Kalpaz Publications*, for the new version of this book. I am certain that the book will benefit researchers, students and readers of RK Narayan!

Someone said, “What a reckless man you are! **Who are you?**”

“You are asking a profound question. I’ve no idea who I am! All my life I have been trying to find the answer. Are you sure you know who you are?” (*A Tiger for Malgudi*, 118)

Let us begin to find out.

Dr S Anandalakshmy, while reading the *Introductory* and *Concluding* chapters of this book, questioned me, *Why have you used the word 'man'? Why not male protagonists?*

My answer to her was what my Guide, Dr Rita Garg, had reiterated:

> In English literature, the word 'male' can be used for any male- insect, bird or an animal. However, if human species is the area of study, the word *Man/Woman* should be used. For example, in the novel *A Tiger for Malgudi*, the protagonist is a Tiger. Instead, his Master, a human, is the 'man' protagonist for this study.

Introduction

A book on the novels of R.K. Narayan (1906 – 2001). The statement itself seems overflowing with information- a rather saturated ground, most people in the field of English Literature would agree. The works of R.K. Narayan, in his writing career of over sixty years, have been a topic of deliberation and study by eminent writers, educationists and professors. In the present scenario, many scholarly studies and research have been undertaken on R.K. Narayan's extensive works. The classical work by William Walsh (1982) makes generous and apt use of quotations from Narayan's works, traces his artistic development and brings into clear relief, the qualities that characterise his fiction, for example, gentle irony, humour and a tolerance of human foibles. Walsh refers to Narayan's writings as 'comedies of sadness' (Walsh: 7).

This book, however, is not only about his novels. It also involves discovering one's identity and pondering over the *self*. Each person has an identity which is the resultant effect of many factors, genetic and otherwise. The personality of an individual is also a product of his/her relationships. In chapter 5, Verse 13, of *The Gita*, Krishna describes the human body as a city with nine gates- two eyes, two ears, two nostrils, one mouth, one anus and one genital. A relationship involves two bodies, two people, the self and the other - eighteen gates in all. That *The Gita* has eighteen sections, that it seeks to make sense of the eighteen books of the *Mahabharata*— which tells the story of a war between family and friends fought over eighteen days involving eighteen armies—indicates that the core teaching of *The Gita* has much to do with relationships. It serves the needs of the householder rather than the hermit (Devdutt Pattanaik).

R.K. Narayan, in his novels, writes about people and their affiliation to others. His characters go through their journey of life, living in the fictional town of *Malgudi*. Narayan's protagonists express themselves through their respective attachment in relationships. Their interdependence on each other, as they live in joint family systems, their association to the family ties and rituals, customs and traditions, get highlighted when Narayan involves them in occupations such as school-teachers, poets, printers, householders, money-vendors or office-goers.

What better way then, than to embark on a journey of reading R.K. Narayan's novels, studying his men protagonists, their diverse relationships and in the process discovering the *self.* Hence this book fulfils, not only the academic responsibility of researching a new area in literature, but also the duty of realisation of 'I' in a world which, despite the growth of technology and awareness, is groping with issues of loss of patience, violence, corruption and dishonesty.

In the *Bhagvad Gita*, Lord Krishna talks about the three *Gunas* (modes of instinct or nature) that are 'installed' in all beings. These modes of nature (or *Gunas)* are *Sattva* (wisdom), *Rajas* (passion) and *Tamas* (darkness). All *jivas* (souls) and their activities in the universe are bound to nature by these three modes. The ratio of these modes in an individual forms his/her temperament. The quality of goodness (*Sattva*) is characterised by purity, wisdom, happiness, spirituality and health. The mode of passion (*Rajas*) is marked by action, desire, lust, attachment and ambition. Darkness (*Tamas*) is identified by destruction, delusion, disease, ignorance and stupor.

In this context, it is interesting to study the *dynamics of modes of nature in the men protagonists of Narayan's novels,* an area which is unexplored so far. It is precisely this lacuna that this book wishes to fill. While previous studies on Narayan have acknowledged that some of his greatest characters are reborn through some kind of spiritual and secular transformation in the course of the novel, this understanding is not extended to exploring the Modes of Nature which also emerge in the process. This book, therefore, explores a tantalizingly new dimension in the writings of Narayan. However, it must be stressed that all three modes of nature and their expressions through the men protagonists of Narayan's novels, are not 'pure' categories, closed in separate boxes. The emphasis here is to see the *influence* of one particular *Guna* in each man protagonist, under particular contexts and circumstances.

All three *Gunas* exist in and surround all beings, but they vary in their relative expressions and degrees. A *Guna* can be increased or decreased through the interaction and influence of external objects, lifestyle practices, thoughts and actions. Further, sometimes these *Gunas* intermingle and flow into each other, with no neat dividing lines. Each mode of nature has its own characteristics. Since the external world and the internal world of the mind are made of matter, the qualities of the three *Gunas* are seen in both. For example, in the external world *Sattva* is seen as equilibrium and serenity, *Rajas* as dynamism and movement while *Tamas* as inertia and stagnancy. In the internal world of the mind, *Sattva* is experienced as compassion, wisdom, knowledge and kindness, *Rajas* as desire, attachment, hyperactivity, fear, obedience, power, prestige and *Tamas* as impurity, greed, anger, envy, delusion and lack of self-control (Pattanaik). Eating habits are also highlighted according to the three Modes of Nature (*Gunas*). The food one intakes can be used as a sign of the predominating inherent mode. *Sattvik* mode implies health-conscious consumption of food including items like fruits, vegetables, cereals and dairy products. *Rajasic* food is attached to sense gratification whereas food which is *Tamasic* is stale, under-ripe or over-ripe, canned, reheated or fermented. Eating too much is also a characteristic trait of the predominant *Tamas Guna.*

The dynamics, intermingling and predominance of any mode of nature in the multifaceted men characters of Narayan's novels thus lends itself to complex readings. Further, though his novels have etched fascinating women characters, the book concentrates on the men protagonists, as they often provide the backbone of his works. Reading and re-reading R.K. Narayan's all fifteen novels several times enabled me to segregate the men protagonists into three categories, each under the impact of one highlighting mode of nature – *Sattva*, *Rajas* or *Tamas.*

1

Amalgamating Themes

Rasipuram Krishnaswami Iyer Narayanaswami

(October 10th, 1906 – May 13th, 2001)

R. K. Narayan, as the world lovingly knows him, is one of the three leading figures of early Indian literature. His contribution to Indian writing in English fiction sprang over many decades, till his death in 2001. Narayan's writing skill is simple and unpretentious, with a natural element of humour in it. It focuses on ordinary people, reminding the readers of their next-door neighbours, relatives and friends. Many novels are set in the fictitious town of 'Malgudi', which helps the reader vividly understand the Indian ethos. Malgudi may be a fictional semi-urban town in southern India, but with characters, each with their respective attitudes and preferences. The works of this great writer, particularly his novels, have been a subject of scholarly interest.

R. K. Narayan was born in Chennai. His father's job required frequent moves and so Narayan spent an important part of his childhood with his maternal grandmother. Later, Narayan moved to Mysore and it is here that he started writing. After completing high school, Narayan failed the university entrance examination and spent a year at home reading and writing. It took Narayan four years to obtain his Bachelor's degree. He held a job as a school teacher but quit in protest when the headmaster of the school asked him to substitute for the physical training master. The experience made Narayan realise that the only career for him was in writing. In 1930, Narayan wrote his first novel, *Swami and Friends*. With this book, Narayan created his fictional town 'Malgudi'. In 1933, Narayan met, fell in love with and married the fifteen-year-old Rajam. Earlier, Narayan had sent the manuscript of *Swami and Friends* to a friend in Oxford, and about this time, the friend showed the manuscript to Graham Greene. Greene recommended the book to his publisher, and it was published in 1935. Narayan's next novel *The Bachelor of Arts* (1937), was inspired in part by his experiences at college and was published by a different publisher, again at the recommendation of Greene. His third novel, *The Dark Room* (1938) was about domestic disharmony and was published by yet another publisher. This book received good reviews.

In the year 1939, Narayan's wife, Rajam, died of typhoid. Her death affected Narayan deeply and he remained depressed for a long time. The bereavement brought about a significant change in his life and was the inspiration behind his next novel, *The English Teacher* (1945). After *The English Teacher*, Narayan's writings took a more imaginative style compared to the semi-autobiographical note of the earlier novels. His next effort, *Mr. Sampath* (1949), was the first book exhibiting this modified approach. Soon after, he published *The Financial Expert* (1952), considered to be his masterpiece and hailed as one of the most original works of fiction. The next novel, *Waiting for the Mahatma* (1955) loosely based on a fictional visit to Malgudi by Mahatma Gandhi, deals with the protagonist's romantic feelings for a woman, when he attends the discourses of the visiting Mahatma. After the wedding of his daughter in 1956, Narayan began travelling occasionally and continued to write. *The Guide* was written while he was visiting the United States in 1956 on the Rockefeller Fellowship. On his return to India, *The Guide* was published. The book won him the Sahitya Akademi Award in 1958.

Narayan's next novel, *The Man-Eater of Malgudi*, was published in 1961. Narayan's next published work was the 1967 novel, *The Vendor of Sweets. The Painter of Signs* (1977) is a bit longer than a novella and makes a marked change from Narayan's other works, as he deals with hitherto unaddressed subjects such as sex. In 1983, Narayan published his next novel, *A Tiger for Malgudi*, about a tiger and its relationship with humans. His next novel, *Talkative Man,* published in 1986, is the tale of an aspiring journalist from Malgudi. In 1990, he published his next novel, *The World of Nagaraj,* also set in Malgudi. Soon after he finished the novel, Narayan fell ill and moved to Madras to be close to his daughter's family. A few years after his move, in 1994, his daughter died and his granddaughter, Bhuvaneswari, started taking care of him in addition to managing his publishing house, *Indian Thought Publications*. Narayan then published his final book, *Grandmother's Tale.* The book is an autobiographical novella, about his great-grandmother who travelled far and wide to find her husband, who ran away shortly after their marriage. The story was narrated to him by his grandmother, when he was a child.

Narayan is regarded as one of the greatest writers of the twentieth century. Narayan won numerous awards during the course of his literary career. His first major award was in 1958, the Sahitya Academy Award for *The Guide.* In 1964, he received the Padma Bhushan. In 1980, he was awarded the AC Benson Medal by the (British) Royal Society of Literature, of which he was an honorary member. In 1982, he was elected an honorary member of the American Academy of Arts and Letters. He was nominated for the Nobel Prize in Literature multiple times, but never won the honour. Recognition also came in the form of honorary doctorates by the University of Leeds (1967), the University of Mysore (1976) and University of Delhi (1973). Towards the end of his career, Narayan was nominated to the upper house of the Indian Parliament for a six-year term starting in 1989, for his contributions to Indian literature. A year before his death, in 2001, he was awarded India's second-highest civilian honour, the Padma Vibhushan. In May 2001, Narayan was hospitalised. A few hours before he was put on a ventilator, he was planning on writing his next novel, a story about a grandfather. However, Narayan did not get better and never started the novel. He died on May 13, 2001, in Chennai at the age of ninety-four.

Narayan has written stories about people, their emotions and their relationships. He has portrayed the lives and feelings of students, teachers, parents, grandparents, journalists, artists, financiers, film-makers and movie stars. This makes his characters universal. Seeing the deep preponderance of spirituality, tradition, *dharma* and *karma* in Narayan's novels, it is fascinating to explore where, why and how modes of nature (*Gunas)* are reflected in his protagonists and characters.

While there is immense research on the novels of Narayan, the implications of the three *Gunas* on the men protagonists of his novels have not yet been explored.

The Modes of Nature (*Gunas*)

In the *Bhagvad Gita*, Lord Krishna talks about the three *Gunas* (modes of nature)- *Sattva* (wisdom), *Rajas* (passion) and *Tamas* (darkness) which are present in all beings. The word *Guna* in Sanskrit has many uses, but here, in the context of the three *Gunas*, it refers to the 'qualities', 'modes' or 'phases' of matter. Matter is composed of eight basic elements- earth, water, fire, air, space, mind, intellect and identity. The first five elements comprise the gross aspects of matter and the last three elements comprise the subtle aspects of matter. The characteristics of these eight material elements develop according to the three modes, the *Gunas*.

The mode of goodness (*Sattva*) is characterised by goodness, wisdom, purity, illumination, order, stability, permanence, happiness, spirituality, cleanliness and health. The mode of passion (*Rajas*) is indicated by action, creation, desire, lust, attachment, movement and strife. Darkness (*Tamas*) is portrayed by destruction, disease, ignorance, intoxication and sleep.

Food in the mode of goodness includes fresh salads, milk, fruits and nuts; in the mode of passion, is cooked, spicy and stimulating. Food in the mode of darkness is derived from pain, fermentation and is stale and rancid.

Animals in the quality of goodness are peaceful and productive such as the cow, horse and elephant. A monkey, a cat, a dog are animals in the mode of passion. Snakes, lizards, scorpions and bats are examples of animals in the condition of darkness.

The cultivation of knowledge which leads to prosperity and peace is in the modes of goodness and passion. Knowledge leading to weapons of mass destruction is in the mode of darkness. A house which is dark, full of fights and filth is a home in the mode of darkness. One that is illuminated, is peaceful, orderly and clean is a home in the mode of goodness.

Most people live their lives neither in full goodness nor in full darkness and so the mode of passion is the most prominent mode. All aspects of life can be analysed according to these three modes of nature. This is an important part of the Hindu way of seeing the universe. All the three *Gunas* mostly remain together, although at any given time, one of these qualities predominates over the other two.

The Bhagvad Gita, considered as part of the sixth book of *The Mahabharata*, is the central text of Hinduism. It is a philosophical dialogue between Lord Krishna and the warrior Arjuna. *The Gita* discusses selflessness, duty, devotion and meditation. The *Bhagvad Gita* (Song of the Lord) consists of seven hundred verses, divided into eighteen chapters. Arjuna expresses his unwillingness to engage in a war against his friends and relatives. Krishna exhorts Arjuna to do his duty as a warrior, to fight and kill. Krishna then explains the nature of the soul and the proper way to reach God. Shri Krishna's discourse to Arjun based on the three *Gunas* is as follows:

> Sattva, Rajas and Tamas, —these Gunas, O mighty-armed, born of Prakriti, bind fast in the body the indestructible embodied one. (Verse 5)
>
> Of these Sattva, from its stainlessness luminous and free from evil, binds, O sinless one, by attachment to happiness and by attachment to knowledge. (Verse 6)
>
> Know Rajas to be of the nature of passion, giving rise to thirst and attachment; it binds fast, O son of Kunti, the embodied one, by attachment to action. (Verse 7)
>
> And know Tamas to be born of ignorance, stupefying all embodied beings; it binds fast, O descendant of Bharata, by miscomprehension, indolence and sleep. (Verse 8)
>
> Sattva attaches to happiness and Rajas to action, O descendant of Bharata; while Tamas, verily, shrouding discrimination, attaches to miscomprehension. (Verse 9)
>
> Sattva arises, O descendant of Bharata, predominating over Rajas and Tamas; and Rajas over Sattva and Tamas; so, Tamas over Sattva and Rajas. (Verse 10)

When through every sense in this body, the light of intelligence shines, then it should be known that Sattva is predominant. (Verse 11)

Greed, activity, the undertaking of actions, unrest, longing—these arise when Rajas is predominant, O bull of the: Bharatas. (Verse 12)

Darkness, inertness, miscomprehension and delusion, —these arise when Tamas is predominant, O descendant of Kuru. (Verse 13)

If the embodied one meets death when Sattva is predominant, then he attains to the spotless regions of the worshippers of the Highest. (Verse 14)

Meeting death in Rajas he is born among those attached to action; so dying in Tamas, he is born in the wombs of the irrational. (Verse 15)

The fruit of good action, they say, is Sattvika and pure; verily, the fruit of Rajas is pain and ignorance is the fruit of Tamas. (Verse 16)

From Sattva arises wisdom and greed from Rajas; miscomprehension, delusion and ignorance arise from Tamas. (Verse 17)

The Sattva-abiding go upwards; the Rajasika dwell in the middle; and the Tamasika, abiding in the function of the lowest Guna, go downwards. (Verse 18)

When the seer beholds no agent other than the Gunas and knows that which is higher than the Gunas, he attains to My being. (Verse 19)

The embodied one having gone beyond these three Gunas out of which the body is evolved, is freed from birth, death, decay and pain and attains to immortality. (Verse 20)

Arjuna said:

By what marks, O Lord, is he (known) who has gone beyond these three Gunas? What is his conduct and how does he pass beyond these three Gunas? (Verse 21)

The Blessed Lord said:

He who hates not the appearance of light (the effect of Sattva), activity (the effect of Rajas) and delusion (the effect of Tamas), (in his own mind), O Pandava, nor longs for them when absent. (Verse 22)

He who, sitting like one unconcerned, is moved not by the Gunas, who, knowing that the Gunas operate, is Self-centred and swerves no. (Verse 23)

Alike in pleasure and pain, self-abiding, regarding a clod of earth, a stone and gold alike; the same to agreeable and disagreeable, firm, the same in censure and, praise. (Verse 24)

The same in honour and disgrace, the same to friend and foe, relinquishing all undertakings—he is said to have gone beyond the Gunas. (Verse 25)

And he who serves Me with an unswerving devotion, he, going beyond the Gunas, is fitted for becoming Brahman. (Verse 26)

For I am the abode of Brahman, the Immortal and Immutable, of everlasting Dharma and of Absolute Bliss. (Verse 27)

In the Mahabharata, (Aswamedha Parva, Sections XXXVI to XXXIX) Brahma (the Grandsire Prajapati) says:

Darkness should be known to have the night (or obscurity) for its essence. It is otherwise called Delusion. It has unrighteousness (or sin) also for its indication and it is always present in all sinful acts.

The true nature of their characteristics will now be declared by me with reasons.

Tamas (Darkness)

Complete delusion, ignorance, indecision in respect of action, sleep, haughtiness, fear, grief, censure of good acts, loss of memory, rashness of judgment, absence of faith, violation of all rules of conduct, want of discrimination, blindness, vileness of behaviour, boastful assertions of performance when there has been no performance, presumption of knowledge in ignorance, unfriendliness (or hostility), evilness of disposition, absence of faith, stupid reasoning, crookedness, incapacity for association, sinful action, senselessness, stolidity, lassitude, absence of self-control, degradation, - all these qualities are known as belonging to Darkness (*Tamas*).

Rajas (Passion)

Brahma said: I shall now declare to you accurately what the quality of Passion (*Rajas)* is.

Injuring others, beauty, toil, pleasure and pain, cold and heat, lordship (or power), war, peace, arguments, dissatisfaction, endurance, might, valour, pride, wrath, exertion, quarrel, jealousy, desire, malice, battle, the sense of mine, protection of others, slaughter, bonds and affliction, buying and selling, cutting, piercing and cutting off the coat that another has worn, fierceness, cruelty, vilifying, pointing out the faults of others, thoughts entirely devoted to worldly affairs, anxiety, animosity, reviling of others, false speech, false or vain gifts, doubt, boastfulness of speech, praise and criticisms, laudation, prowess, defiance, attendance (as on the weak and the sick), obedience (to the commands of preceptors and parents), service or ministrations, harbouring of thirst or desire, cleverness or dexterity of conduct, policy heedlessness, possessions and diverse decorations that prevail in the world among men, women, animals, inanimate things, houses, grief, incredulousness, vows and regulations, actions with expectation (of good result), diverse acts of public charity, the rites in respect of Swaha salutations, rites of Swadha and Vashat, officiating at the sacrifices of others, imparting of instruction, performance of sacrifices, study, making of gifts, acceptance of gifts, auspicious acts, the wish to have this and that, affection generated by the merits of the object for which or whom it is felt, treachery, deception, disrespect and respect, theft, killing, desire of concealment, vexation, wakefulness, ostentation, haughtiness, attachment, devotion, contentment, exultation, gambling, indulgence in scandal, all relations arising out of women, attachment to dancing, instrumental music and songs – all these qualities have been said to belong to the quality of Passion (*Rajas)*.

Sattva (Goodness)

> Brahma said: Sattva is beneficial to all creatures in the world and constitutes the conduct of those that are good.
>
> Joy, satisfaction, nobility, enlightenment and happiness, absence of stinginess, absence of fear, contentment, disposition for faith, forgiveness, courage, abstention from injuring any creature, equability, truth, straightforwardness, absence of wrath, absence of malice, purity, cleverness, prowess-these appertain to the quality of Goodness (Sattwa). He who is devoted to the duty of Yoga, regarding knowledge to be vain, conduct to be vain, service to be vain and mode of life to be vain, attains to what is highest in the world hereafter. Freedom from the idea of mine, freedom from egoism, freedom from expectations, looking upon all with an equal eye and freedom from desire – these constitute the eternal religion of the good. Confidence, modesty, forgiveness, renunciation, purity, absence of laziness, absence of cruelty, absence of delusion, compassion to all creatures, absence of the disposition to calumniate, exultation, satisfaction, rapture, humility, good behaviour, purity in all acts having for their object the attainment of tranquillity, righteous understanding, emancipation from attachments, indifference, Brahmacharya (celibacy), complete renunciation, freedom from expectations, unbroken observance of righteousness, beliefs that gifts are vain, sacrifices are vain, study is vain, vows are vain, acceptance of gifts is vain, observance of duties is vain and penances are vain – those Brahmanas (priests) in this world, whose conduct is marked by these virtues, who adhere to righteousness, who abide in the Vedas, are said to be wise and possessed of correctness of vision.

All three *Gunas* are present in all beings, but vary in their relative amounts. An individual possesses the unique ability to alter the levels of *Gunas* in body and mind. A *Guna* can be increased or decreased through the interaction and influence of external objects, lifestyle practices, thoughts and emotions. All *Gunas* create attachment and thus bind the *'self'* to the *'ego'*.

When one rises above the three *Gunas*, one is free of birth, old age, disease and death attains enlightenment. *(Bhagvad Gita).*

While previous studies on Narayan have acknowledged that some of his greatest characters are reborn through some kind of spiritual and secular transformation, this understanding is not extended to exploring the modes of nature or characteristics and instincts of man that also emerge in the process. This book, consisting of all his novels, delves into an aspect of his works, which has remained unexamined so far. Thus, it adds a new line to the understanding of Narayan's men protagonists, which so far have been studied only as characters, real or unreal, humane or bad. This book analyses the men protagonists in the novels of R.K. Narayan, each under one highlighting *Guna* (*Sattva, Rajas* or *Tamas*). A new way not only to look at Narayan's men characters, but also trace their responses towards situations and relationships, is in the offing through this book.

2

Predominance of *Sattva Guna*

Novels and Characters

R. K. Narayan's novels, carry within them, explicit and implicit moral values and lay great emphasis on the intrinsic good nature of human beings. In his writings, goodness ultimately triumphs over evil. Deep belief in an ethical and principled value system characterise his novels and their characters. His heroes portray an evolving consciousness, which may begin with a note of uncertainty, turmoil and loneliness, but ends up in certainty, peace and fullness. Combined with this, there is a deep belief in the positive features of the traditional Hindu faith in many of his novels. These attributes have been explored by various scholars, but have not been explicitly classified under the signifying *Sattva Guna*. However, if Narayan's men protagonists are explored under the rubric of *Sattva mode of nature,* a glimpse of additional nuances is noticed. For example, *goodness* combines with *Hindu values*, *optimism* with *compassion*, *wisdom* with *kindness* thus, revealing the deep influence of Hindu texts and scriptures on Narayan. This chapter explores the *Sattva Guna* in the men protagonists of some of Narayan's novels. States Chapter 14 of *Bhagvad Gita:*

> SATTVA is purity. Sattva is light. Sattva is wisdom. Happiness and Sattva stay together. Harmony and Sattva breathe together. The senses in Sattva are surcharged with the light of knowledge. If one leaves the body when Sattva prevails, then to the pure abode of the Sages he goes.

Sattva mode denotes the influence of wisdom and knowledge in thoughts, words and actions. Kindness, compassion and altruism are closely associated with wisdom. Without sympathy and compassion, rationality and reason fail to prevail. Thus, the distinguishing features of the *Sattva Guna* are intermingled. Narayan in his novels, ***Waiting for the Mahatma* (1955), *The Man-Eater of Malgudi* (1961), *The Vendor of Sweets* (1967), *The Painter of Signs* (1976) and *A Tiger for Malgudi* (1983)** portrays his men protagonists in a storyline where the *Sattva Guna* reigns supreme.

Sriram in *Waiting for the Mahatma*

Nataraj in *The Man-Eater of Malgudi*

Jagan in *The Vendor of Sweets*

Raman in *The Painter of Signs*

The Master in *A Tiger for Malgudi* are men protagonists, who show qualities of altruism, empathy, wisdom, kindness, divinity and purity. These men have sympathy towards others, show rationality in their judgements and their actions strongly lean towards Gandhi's doctrine of love and non-violence. They believe in doing their duty according to their belief and faith in religion and spirituality. Thus, they show predominance of *Sattva Guna*. This chapter specifically explores four characteristics specific to *Sattva Guna.*

(a) Wisdom and Knowledge

(b) Compassion

(c) Following the Gandhian Way of Life

(d) Religious bent of Mind and Spirituality through various characters mentioned above. These attributes often intermingle with each other and co-habit with other qualities like truth, non-violence and love.

R. K. Narayan wrote *Waiting for the Mahatma* in 1955, seven years after the assassination of Gandhi. It is essentially a love story of Sriram and Bharti against the backdrop of India's struggle for freedom. Sriram gets attracted to Bharti and this leads him to join Gandhi's movement for independent India. Through the course of the story, Sriram tries to persuade Bharti to marry him. Later, towards the end, he spends some time in jail, while India wakes up to freedom. He is reunited with Bharti, amidst the tragedy of India's partition. The story ends with Gandhi's blessings for their engagement and eventually Gandhi's death. *Waiting for the Mahatma* traces the metamorphosis of Sriram, the man protagonist in the novel, from an immature, weak young man to a thinking individual. His journey in the novel seesaws between impatience and awareness. Sriram comes to understand issues like untouchability, hand spun *khadi* cloth, spirit of nationalism, truth, non-violence and love. This man protagonist, thus, comes under the predominance of the *Sattva Guna*. In shaping his character, Narayan has used values of kindness, patience and understanding of Gandhian values and doctrine of non-violence. Though initially, the character of Sriram cannot be regarded as having qualities predominating the *Sattva Guna*, the way his character evolves in the novel and his dialogues and discussions with others gradually establish how *Sattva Guna* becomes critical in framing of his character.

The chief characteristic of a person under the influence of *Sattva Guna* is that s/he believes in purity of thoughts, words and actions. Md. Rizwan considers Narayan to be 'essentially moral in his attitude towards life... a man of moral conscience' (17). The immense faith that evil is self-destructive and that despite others doing wrong, one must tread the path of empathy, goodness and purity, qualifies Nataraj, the man protagonist in Narayan's novel *The Man-Eater of Malgudi* (1961) to be studied under the *Sattva Guna*. This novel is considered by critics to be one of Narayan's finest works. It is an allegory showing that evil is self-destructive. The title is ironic because the man-eater in the novel is not an animal, but a human being, a man named Vasu. He kills a large number of wild animals in Mempi forests. Vasu is capable of killing another human with a single blow of his strong hammer-fist. The story is narrated in the first person by its protagonist Nataraj, who works as a printer in Malgudi. His life gets disturbed when H. Vasu, a taxidermist (a person who stuffs dead animals to be sold as trophies), comes to stay with him. Vasu is an aggressive man, six feet tall, bull-necked and hammer-fisted, who starts robbing the Mempi forest of its wild life. Soon after, Vasu starts bringing Rangi, a notorious dancing woman, to his room. The crisis, however, comes to a head when Vasu threatens to kill Kumar, the temple elephant, during a procession.

Nataraj is very fond of Kumar and gets very upset. The matter is reported to the police authorities, but they express their inability to take any action against Vasu, until the crime has actually been committed. Nataraj does his best to save Kumar and is surprised when the procession passes by peacefully. The next morning Vasu is found dead in his room. The police authorities start investigations but fail to find any clue. Later it is revealed that while striking a mosquito settled on his forehead, Vasu slapped his temple and died instantaneously. He thus dies of a blow from his own hammer-fist. Nataraj, protagonist of *The Man-Eater of Malgudi* is eligible to come under the *Sattva Guna* not only because of his pure qualities, but also because his character stands in stark contrast to Vasu, who has all the distinctive attributes of the *Tamas Guna* (which I explore in another chapter of the book).

Narayan's novel, *The Vendor of Sweets,* was published in 1967. It is the story of Jagan, a sweet-vendor and his son, Mali. Jagan has a strong religious bent of mind. He is influenced by *Bhagvad Gita* and is a staunch follower of Gandhi. The story portrays the father-son relationship and the tensions caused by the difference of outlook between the older and younger generation. Mali announces his decision to give up his studies to write a novel. Later he leaves for America. Jagan is disturbed when in one of Mali's letters he mentions that he has started eating beef. Events proceed and Mali returns home, not alone, but with his American wife, Grace. Later, Jagan learns, to his great dismay, that they are not actually married, but have been living together. Mali now wants to set up a factory for manufacturing story-writing machines, in collaboration with the Americans. For this he needs two and a half lakh rupees. He presses his father to give him the money because he believes that Jagan has considerable wealth. Events take a turn. Finally, Jagan decides to hand over his business to his son and lead a retired life in an *ashram* across the river. Honesty, compassion, kindness, truth and doing good deeds for others, are virtues in Jagan which qualify him to be examined under the qualities that denote the *Sattva Guna.* Although Jagan is a businessman selling sweets, he is devoted in his service and does not cheat his customers. He is against adulteration and in fact opposes others in the same business when they raise prices of their products. As a father, he is shown to be concerned about his son. Throughout Mali's journey of growing up,

Jagan is anxious that Mali takes the right path, marries the right way and conducts himself in the right manner.

The Painter of Signs, published in 1976, presents a picture of India in the post-independence era. The novel depicts changes in human outlook with regard to cherished ideals, established institutions and accepted values. Both scientific and rational trends are represented by Narayan in the characters of Daisy and the man protagonist Raman. Daisy is a modern independent woman, working on birth-control awareness projects. Raman and Daisy fall in love. In his journey in the novel, Raman's character passes through emotions of tenderness towards his aunt, love and passion for Daisy and finally self-realisation when Daisy leaves him to pursue the demands of her work. Through this novel, Narayan brings to the fore the material advancement on one hand and wide rampant mental impoverishment on the other. This is a satire on the prevailing superstitions of society, besides showcasing the exploitation of gullible women at the hands of self- acclaimed God-men. The novel follows a formula of 'order-disorder-order', making it evident that life never takes a straight course. In the end, Raman realises that true independence and real happiness lies in doing one's own job. Raman's experience with the strong-willed Daisy makes him self-analytical and brings him to a ripe conviction that there are more important things in life than just marriage or a man-woman relationship. Raman's rationale and logic, self-awareness and altruistic behaviour towards Daisy, his sacrifice in letting Daisy go to pursue her career so that she may remain happy and many other similar traits are the prevailing qualities in his disposition which make him eligible in the category of *Sattva Guna.*

A Tiger for Malgudi, which was published in 1983, is a creative novel by Narayan about a tiger who is said to have possessed the soul of an enlightened human being. Narayan justifies the subject in his introduction to the novel:

> "Why tiger? Why not a mouse?" asked a smart journalist who had come to interview me, when I mentioned the subject of my novel. I could only reply, "so that the chief character may not be trampled upon or lost sight of in a hole."

The story fluctuates between flashback and the present time with 'an aged tiger lying in its cage ruminating on its past, beginning with his cub-hood and his wild days in the jungle and later, life in captivity as a circus star' (8). Later the tiger meets a hermit, the Master, who appears to be the mouthpiece of Narayan. He has renounced his family and the comforts and riches of life. In this hermit, Raja, the tiger, finds his friend and teacher. The account of Raja and the Master, travels the circus and the jungle to finally end in separation of the two. The novel is full of various elements of wisdom and truth. The Master has many primary characteristics which ascertain his *Sattva Guna*. His journey of life has matured him into self-awareness and self-identification. He is wise, non-judgemental, kind-hearted and empathetic. He is compassionate and shows affinity towards all forms of life.

Thus, the men protagonists in Narayan's above mentioned five novels show the impact of *Sattva Guna*. It needs to be noted that while the book attempts to delineate and separate the various traits specific to *Sattva Guna*, they often criss-cross and intermingle with each other.

Wisdom and Knowledge

Wisdom is one of the chief qualities of *Sattva Guna*. Wisdom is the ability to think and act, using knowledge, experience, understanding, common sense and insight. Wisdom has been regarded as one of the four cardinal virtues. It is a habit or disposition to perform the action with the highest degree of adequacy under any given circumstance. It implies a possession of knowledge or the seeking thereof in order to apply it to the given circumstance. It involves an understanding of people, things, events, situations and the willingness as well as the ability to apply perception, judgment and action, in keeping with the understanding of what is the optimal course of action. Wisdom in Hinduism is considered a state of mind and soul where a person achieves liberation. In other words, wisdom means a person with self-awareness, as the one who witnesses the entire creation in all its facets and forms.

Knowledge is a familiarity, awareness or understanding of someone or something, such as facts, information, descriptions, or skills, which is acquired through experience or education by perceiving, discovering or learning. It can refer to a theoretical or practical understanding of a subject. It can be implicit (as with practical skill or expertise) or explicit (as with the theoretical understanding of a subject); it can be informal or systematic. The philosopher Plato famously defined knowledge as 'justified true belief'. There are other explanations and theories to understand knowledge. Knowledge acquisition involves complex cognitive processes: perception, communication and reasoning. Moreover, knowledge sharing or distribution, which is also known as *vidya daan*, is a major tenet of all religions. The God of intellect (wisdom) is *Ganesha* and the goddess of knowledge is *Saraswati*. One of the Sanskrit verses, which combine knowledge and wisdom is:

om asato maa sad-gamaya; tamaso
maa jyotir-ga-maya; mrtyor-maa
amrutam gamaya. om shaantih
shaantih shaantih.

[O Lord lead me from the unreal to the real.
Lead me from darkness to light.
Lead me from death to immortality.
May there be peace, peace and perfect peace]
(*Brihadaranyaka Upanishad* 1.3.28).

It needs to be stated that truth is an integral part of wisdom and knowledge. Let me explicate the *Sattva* characteristics of wisdom and knowledge, combined with truth, through some of the men protagonists of Narayan.

The novel *Waiting for the Mahatma* epitomises the *Sattva Guna* of wisdom and knowledge through the Gandhian way of life, reflected in its man protagonist Sriram. He comes under the guidance and influence of Gandhi, who is wise and knowledgeable. Sriram has shades of *Sattva Guna* in the beginning when he questions as to 'why anything should be concealed from anyone?' (12). The values of truth, non-violence, respect for all castes and patriotism dawn on him when he comes in contact with Mahatma Gandhi, who visits his town Malgudi.

Digambar Singh Dewari states:

As Gandhian thought presents experimental truth, Narayan's fiction also presents imaginative truth. The imaginary town of Malgudi which presents a fictional background to Narayan's novels is rightly viewed by G. J. V. Prasad as "less a place and more a point of view". Though the topography of Malgudi also expands as Narayan's career as a novelist matures, Narayan is least concerned in presenting literal truth (103).

Dhananjay Tripathi, writing on Phenomenology and Consciousness in R.K. Narayan's novels is of the view:

> *Waiting for the Mahatma* is very significant because it helps to demolish the myth that Narayan escapes the social reality.... (It) provides ample scope for phenomenological reading.... (and) is a full-scale portrayal of the author's consciousness of the Gandhian movement (206-7).
>
> Mahatma Gandhi's wisdom gets echoed when Sriram says, "Yes, Bapuji, I will be a different man", to which Gandhiji replies, "why do you say "different"? You will be all right if you are fully yourself" (68).

Throughout the novel, Narayan makes Sriram hear the discourses of Gandhi and makes Sriram reflect on and internalise 'that there must be a great deal in what he says. We always think that we are superior people. How granny bullies that ragged scavenger who comes to our house every day to sweep our backyard!' (30-1). Initially though Sriram joins Gandhi's movement for independence due to his attraction for Bharti, later he comes on his own and shows independent thinking, an ingredient linked closely to *Sattva Guna.* He says, "Even the British government could not make me do what I didn't want to" (198). In this journey of finding himself, he goes to the jail, is released in free India and finally witnesses the Mahatma's assassination. K. Chellapan states:

> Narayan's characters are literary incarnations of the Gandhian ideal. They are people in quest of truth. They embody the greatest virtues of the Hindu way of life at the level of the man in the street; exactly where Gandhi wanted them to be.

In Narayan's novel *The Man-Eater of Malgudi,* wisdom and knowledge shine in Nataraj's disposition. The constant contrast and comparison between Nataraj and Vasu, each symbolic of *Sattva Guna* and *Tamas Guna* respectively, is able to stress the importance of wisdom. Through his beautiful one-line dialogues between the two characters, this is brought out sharply. For example, at one place Vasu says, "I never forget". Nataraj replies, "and I never remember" (19). Deep philosophical message is depicted thus. To never remember a hurt, hold a grievance, to forget an insult and to forgive unconditionally are essential qualities of the *Sattva Guna*. Nataraj is contented and not greedy. He helps Vasu by offering him a room to stay, but is not a landlord and does not want to be one. Besides, he is wise. In his words, "As a man of education, Vasu, you should not shut your mind to new ideas." Analysing the wisdom and maturity displayed by Nataraj and his contrasting with Vasu, William Walsh states:

> In the contrast between Nataraj and Vasu, in the more and more frantic and frightened efforts of Nataraj to oppose Vasu, we see how Narayan writes within a settled scheme. The mode of belief, the inheritance and the characteristic reaction to the social and physical environment — all these recur in his novels. They are the conditions of the civilisation Narayan seems to embody and interpret. It is true, too, that the central predicament of the characters reappears in novel after novel, but the solution adopted by his protagonists, the particular escape from the precise predicament and the conditions in which it takes place – these are different from novel to novel and show themselves of a human experience which is inexhaustible in its content and significance (ed. Srinath: 152).

Animosity, anger and resentment are feelings which reflect the *Tamas Guna*, which I explicate in another chapter. If a person has an awareness, understanding, knowledge and wisdom that harbouring such feelings is self-destructive, s/he will try to overcome them. The same happens to Nataraj. He is seen reflecting:

> I could never be a successful enemy to anyone. Any enmity worried me night and day. As a schoolboy I persistently shadowed around the one person with whom I was supposed to be on terms of hate and hostility. I felt acutely uneasy as long as our enmity lasted. I was never more than a few paces away from him as we started home from school. I sat on a bench immediately behind him and tried to attract his attention by coughing and clearing my throat or

> by brushing against his back while picking up a pencil deliberately dropped on the floor. I made myself abject in order to win a favourable look or word from my enemy and waited for a chance to tell him that I wanted to be friends with him. It bothered me like a toothache. I was longing for a word with Vasu. I stood like a child at the treadle, hoping he would look at me and nod and that all would be well again. He was terrible specimen of human being no doubt, but I wanted to be on talking terms with him. This was a complex mood. I couldn't say that I liked him or approved of anything he said or did, but I didn't want to be repulsed by him. My mind seethed with plans as to how to re-establish cordiality (92).

Vasu believes in the philosophy that 'science conquers nature in a new way each day; why not in creation also? (15). This, Nataraj does not accept because he wisely believes in the superiority of nature. He does not like it when he hears Vasu talking about his teacher in a degrading manner and is quick to check him with his sensible wisdom, "After all he taught you to be strong – he was your guru…He also gave you six eggs a day and – how much milk and almonds was it?" (17). There are many quotes of wisdom that are reflected in this novel, for example that 'time and tide wait for none', which has undertones of raising the self and acquiring qualities which tilt towards the *Sattva Guna.* This Narayan applies beautifully in the way he brings about Vasu's end. States Nityananda Pattnayak:

> Continuity in time is reinforced in *The Man-Eater of Malgudi* taking cue from the Indian myths and using mythical characters in it. Vasu, the modern version of bhasmasura is crushed under the wheels of time; time is least concerned about his physical powers, about his knowledge power. The hands of the clock in his room move on, least touching the drama of Malgudi life ruffled by the threats of Vasu. Vasu had set his alarm clock to arouse him from the deep sleep but, during the period, his death occurred and the author tells how time is not at all bothered about this important event in the temporal world of Malgudi, "the alarm clock which had screeched in the dark on the previous night was now ticking away modestly. Its pale pink patch must have watched the process of Vasu's death" (221).

Thus, time is a mute witness to the rise and fall of Vasu (93). Overall, it can be said that Nataraj's disposition shows the predominance of *Sattva Guna*. In his wisdom he realises that all forms of life should be respected and thus makes an effort to save Kumar from being killed at the hands of Vasu. Since Vasu dies due to a blow to his temple by his own hammer-fist, Nataraj emerges a winner with the knowledge that evil is self-destructive. Being satisfied with one self in any given set of circumstances is a sovereign quality of the *Sattva Guna*.

In the novel, *The Vendor of Sweets*, Jagan's words, "Do you realise how few ever really understand how fortunate they are in their circumstances?" (26) are full of wisdom. Jagan believes in dignity of labour and so once when his son Mali asks him to engage a cook, he retorts with "do we engage a servant to do the breathing for us?" (24). Jagan does not believe in blame games. Rather he wants everyone to take personal responsibility for growth and development. He says, "Why do you blame the country for everything? It has been good enough for four hundred millions" (88). Jagan also believes in the philosophy that money earned for need, to make ends meet, leads to happiness and contentment. However, money earned for greed leads to lust, jealousy, unhappiness, hatred and strained inter-personal relationships. This shows tremendous wisdom in Jagan's thinking. He considers money to be evil and believes that one is 'happier without it. It is enough if an activity goes on self-supported; no need to earn money' (92). Jagan's philosophy of *Sattva Guna,* filled with wisdom and knowledge, is reflected in his thoughts. He maintains that 'even when one wants to make profits, one should retain some sense of service. What would one do with many mansions?' (70). In his wisdom, he quotes a Tamil verse which says that even if eighty million ideas float across your mind, you cannot wear more than four cubits of cloth or eat more than a little measure of rice at a time (70). He does 'not like the idea of cheating his customers' (80) and also 'performs his charity without question' (83). In his words:

> I wanted to serve the public in my own way by making available pure sweets, particularly for poor children. If others want to eat sweets, they must have the purest ones that is all. I am thinking particularly of children and poor people (91).

Laying stress on contentment and showing wisdom, Narayan asserts in *The Vendor of Sweets*:

> Cousin tells Jagan, "Every gift of life you are blessed with: what ninety out of hundred people crave for — money; and what hundred out of hundred people crave for – contentment. Yet you have not mastered one thing, that's the art of looking happy. You are always looking careworn (43).

The knowledge and wisdom reflected in Jagan's words cement the predominance of *Sattva Guna* in his character. His wisdom and respect for knowledge is highlighted when he says, "Didn't you tell him that books must be treated respectfully, being a form of the Goddess Saraswati?" (30). He again states, "Light rays should soothe the optic nerves and not stimulate them" (124). His words, "At first don't hurry, but when you decide, be swift and positive" bring out wise thoughts. At another place he says, "We are blinded by our attachments. Every attachment creates a delusion and we are carried away by it" (132). Knowledge of diverse cultures, practices, customs and rituals should lead to filtering out whatever one does not agree with. This is possible only when one acts under the influence of *Sattva Guna* of wisdom and self-awareness. Blindly following another country's cultures or customs can lead to confusion and delusion. P. K. Singh, while critically evaluating Narayan's novels, states:

> The east and west encounter is remarkably visible in the novel. The westernised modern India is set against the traditional India. Narayan is aware of the fact that a good number of young men who go to America return with westernised thinking having a motif to ignore their traditions and customs.... The crisis of values in the Hindu joint-family life can well be identified with the clash of the two generations (56).

The man protagonist, Raman in *The Painter of Signs,* is shown to have traits bearing the *Sattva Guna* of knowledge at the very beginning of the novel when he is 'determined to establish the Age of Reason':

> I want a rational explanation for everything, he cries, otherwise my mind refuses to accept any statement.... I am a rationalist and I don't do anything unless I see some logic in it (5).

He is a painter of sign-boards and one day while commuting, he buys wisdom in the form of a message by a professor. When he unfolds the piece of paper containing the town hall Professor's message, it reads "This will pass." The novel states:

> He studied the message and its significance seemed to deepen while he brooded over it, giving him a feeling of perpetually gliding away from objects and movements. Losing all sense of stagnation, Raman felt suddenly light at heart (27).

Raman believes in the wisdom of *shastras*. This can also be due to the fact that since childhood he has stayed with his grandmother. Thus, he understands that 'When one meets a great soul and hears his talk, one attains merit, so say the shastras!' (75). The character of Raman shows tremendous wisdom in the way his understanding about man-woman relationship evolves. Being at an age when he can get attracted to women, when his libido is at its peak, he wishes to establish that the man-woman relationship is not inevitable and that there are other more important things to do in life than marrying' (45). On a lighter note, Narayan writes: 'He had steeled himself against this blunder committed by human beings since Adam. If Adam had possessed a firm mind, the entire course of creation would have taken a different turn' (45). However, Raman gets attracted to Daisy, a social worker, as he spends more and more time in her company and gets a chance to know her closely. Once, while travelling, he wants to get intimate with Daisy. As chance would have it, she is not inside the cart but up on a tree to save herself from a tiger. The next day Raman realises his folly and thanks Daisy for saving him 'from myself' (96). He falls in love with her. Daisy lives with him for a while but realises that her career is her first priority. She wants to leave Raman. *Sattva Guna* shines in Raman's character when after a while he lets her leave him. There is no feeling of desperation, revenge or jealousy. Perhaps a sense of comfort in telling himself that 'maybe we will live together in our next *janma*' (183). Because of his wisdom, Raman becomes practical in his approach to life and retreats to the most frequented place, the Boardless, 'that solid, real world of sublime souls who minded their own business' (183).

In his novel, *A Tiger for Malgudi,* Narayan uses his creativity superbly. He makes an animal, a tiger his mouthpiece. Narayan portrays the tiger on the possible assumption that "he has only the appearance of a tiger, but he is not one.... Inside he is no different from you and me" (146). Since the novel is an autobiographical account of the tiger Raja, Narayan's perception of the *Sattva Guna* of 'need vs greed', even in animals comes on board when he makes Raja say, "Tigers attack only when they feel hungry, unlike human beings who slaughter one another without purpose or hunger" (117). The protagonist in this novel, *The Master*, is portrayed by Narayan as a man who has attained knowledge and wisdom. He does not believe in addressing any form of life as a beast. In Raja's words, "My Master pushed his way through the crowds and admonished, 'Never use the words *beast* or *brute*'. They're ugly words coined by man in his arrogance. The human being thinks all other creatures are beasts". Awful word!' (117). The entire conundrum of life is addressed by Narayan in a powerful conversation, involving the Master:

> Someone said, "What a reckless man you are! Who are you?" "You are asking a profound question. I've no idea who I am! All my life I have been trying to find the answer. Are you sure you know who you are?" (118).

Towards the end of the novel when Raja is down-spirited, confused and is hesitant to leave his Master, the latter says:

> Listen attentively: My past does not exist for me, nor a future. I live for the moment and that awareness is enough for me. To attain this state, I have gone through much hardship, I don't have to explain all that now. I have erased from my mind my name and identity and all that it implies. It would be unthinkable to slide back. You must live your own life and leave me to live mine and end it my own way (171).

The Master's wisdom gets reflected when he warns his wife of yesteryears and that she would have to pass through the jungle all alone. When she replies, "I can go alone, as I came," the Master replies, "Yes, we come into the world alone and are alone while leaving. Your understanding is becoming deeper" (172). Old age is considered as a time which is dreaded by all human beings, since it signifies helplessness and dependency on others. It is a phase when beauty and health bid farewell and the value of a person get diminished. However, the Master gives a new dimension to this thought. He says to Raja:

> Raja, old age has come on you. Beautiful old age, when faculties are dimmed one by one, so that we may be restful, very much like extinguishing lights in a home, one by one, before one goes to sleep. Listen attentively. You may live a maximum of five years; I don't think we should risk your suffering starvation or attack from other creatures or hunters. Once they know you are old and weak, they will come for you and you are going to be alone because we are about to part (174).

The Master explains his philosophy:

> No relationship, human or other, or association of any kind could last forever. Separation is the law of life right from the mother's womb. One has to accept it if one has to live in God's plans (174).

Finally, he prophesises to the tiger: "Both of us will shed our forms soon and perhaps we could meet again, who knows. So goodbye for the present" (176). When reflecting on knowledge and wisdom, the philosopher Bertrand Russell states:

> There are, I think, several factors that contribute to wisdom. Of these I should put first a sense of proportion: the capacity to take account of all the important factors in a problem and to attach to each its due weight.... There must be, also, a certain awareness of the ends of human life.... It is not only in public ways, but in private life equally, that wisdom is needed... It is needed in the choice of ends to be pursued and in emancipation from personal prejudice.... I think the essence of wisdom is emancipation, as far as possible, from the tyranny of the here and now.

We can see that in multiple and different ways, the above men protagonists of Narayan portray these qualities and reflect the *Sattva Guna* of **Wisdom and Knowledge.**

Compassion

Compassion is a predominating qualities of *Sattva Guna*. Compassion is the emotion one feels in response to the suffering of others. It motivates a desire to help. Compassion is often regarded as having an emotional aspect to it, though when based on cerebral notions such as fairness, justice and interdependence, it may be considered rational in nature and its application understood as an activity based on sound judgment. Sympathy is the perception, understanding and reaction to distress or need of another human being. Sympathy is believed to be based on the principle of 'the powerful helping the vulnerable (young, elderly, sick)'. Sympathy is a feeling of care and understanding for someone in need. It is an empathic concern, a feeling of compassion or concern for another, the wish to see them better off or happier.

The etymology of 'compassion' is Latin, meaning 'co-suffering', commonly giving rise to an active desire to alleviate another's suffering. In ethical terms, the expression 'do to others what you would have them do to you' embodies the principle of compassion. In classical literature of Hinduism, compassion is a virtue with many shades, each shade explained by different terms. The three most common terms or traits in this regard are *daya*, *karuna* and *anukampa*. Compassion encompasses all living beings, including those who are strangers and those who are foes. It is what makes it a noble virtue. Tulsidas contrasts *daya* (compassion) with *abhiman* (arrogance, contempt of others), claiming that compassion is a source of *dharmic* life, while arrogance a source of sin. *Daya* is not *kripa* (pity) in Hinduism, or feeling sorry for the sufferer, because that is marred with condescension. Instead, *daya* is feeling one with the sufferer. Compassion is also the basis for *ahimsa*, a core virtue in Hindu philosophy.

Sympathy is intermeshed with compassion, which together with ethics, lead to altruism. Sympathy is an ethical doctrine which holds that the moral value of an individual's action depends solely on its impact on other individuals, regardless of the consequences on the individual itself. Let me elaborate how this particular *Sattva Guna* is exemplified in men protagonists of Narayan.

In the novel *Waiting for the Mahatma,* Sriram, after coming in contact with Mahatma Gandhi realises the meaning of being compassionate towards others. The issue of untouchability is addressed by Narayan when the narrative states that Mahatma preferred staying in a hut 'belonging to the city sweepers who lived on the banks of the river....These men spent less than tenth of their income on food or clothing, always depending upon mendicancy in their off hours for survival....Their possessions were few; if a cow or a calf died in the city they were called in to carry off the carcass and then the colony at the river's edge brightened up for they held a feast on the flesh of the dead animal and made money out of the hide' (37). In Prakash M. Joshi's words:

> Gandhiji is a character and not a symbol; Narayan points in *Waiting for the Mahatma*... Narayan shows him among the Harijans, villagers, children and the volunteers talking about day-to-day life (62).

The *Sattva Guna* of compassion impacts Sriram. Mahatma Gandhi tells him, "You must look after your granny too, she must have devoted herself to bringing you up" (70). Sriram hears Mahatma Gandhi's speech: "before you aspire to drive the British from this country, you must drive every vestige of violence from your system. Remember that it is not going to be a fight with sticks and knives or guns but only with love" (77). The virtue of compassion gets sparked in Sriram's disposition when he hears the Mahatma say, "you must become so sensitive that it is not possible for you to wear sandals made of the hide of slaughtered animals; you should prefer to go bare-foot rather than wear the hide of an animal killed for your sake... (78).

Later, Sriram is seen telling others, "If you have a photo of Mahatma Gandhi, pray that he may inspire you with reasonable thinking... (109). The *Sattva Guna* of compassion and kindness makes him see people struggling with the salt tax and that 'Mahatma Gandhi has been fighting (for it) .... That he will not rest till the Salt Tax is repealed' (119). The note which he receives from Mahatma Gandhi cements Sriram's belief in truth. The note says: 'your work should be a matter of inner faith. It cannot depend upon what you see or understand. Your conscience should be your guide in every action. Consult it and you won't go wrong. Don't guide yourself by what you see. You should do your duty because your inner voice drives you to do it... (128).

Thus, Sriram understands the *Sattva Guna* of selfless love towards weak and the downtrodden. He comes to realize the value of compassion, truth and non-violence.

In *The Man-Eater of Malgudi*, the man protagonist Nataraj is helpful and kind-hearted. He offers his attic space to Vasu to stay. He gets upset when Vasu portrays Nataraj as a rent-collecting landlord. He is vocal in saying, "I am not a rentier. I let him in as a friend and not as a tenant. Do you want to heap on my head the reputation of being a man who takes rent for his attic space?" (67). *Sattva Guna* of compassion and sympathy is brought to the foray by Narayan when Vasu kills a pet dog in the neighbourhood. Nataraj is disturbed not only because the dog is killed, but also at the agony of the child, Ramu, who owned the dog. He chides himself and also promises himself to help the young fellow:

> I had no time actually to go out and seek a dog for the boy. But I had several plans in my head. I'd make a list of all my friends with dogs, tabulate each breed, note down their breeding time, make one of them promise to give one of the litter to me, make a round of visit every Sunday afternoon and finally pick up a dog for the young fellow. My son asked me at nights while he nestled close to me (when night advanced the fear of the monster grew in him and he refused to sleep in the separate bed), as if he were a sharer of my dream, "Get me a puppy too, father, when you get one for Ramu" (105).

Nataraj's kind heartedness for the elephant, Kumar, surfaces when Kumar falls ill and refuses food (114). Nataraj feels genuinely concerned about Kumar and volunteers to "go and meet this doctor" (115). The protagonist is compassionate towards his wife and wants her to 'go and enjoy' without worrying over him (185). He wants to do all he can to help Kumar saved from the bullet of Vasu. He suggests, "Why not change the route of the procession? Why not drop procession altogether? Or why not leave the elephant out?" (190). He sympathises with the elephant:

> That poor elephant! He was enjoying all the fun today, decorated, happy and playing with the children, starting the day so well. Somehow, he must return to the Goddess on the mountain road, graze in the forests on the blue hills and continue to delight the children in all those villages (207).

Later, towards the end of the novel, Nataraj, the peace loving, non-aggressive man, with qualities of compassion and altruism, goes up the attic to try and foil Vasu's plan of killing the temple-elephant:

> He was still asleep. As my fingers reached the cold butt of his gun, I could have swooned with excitement. I had never touched a gun before and felt scared. I rose to my feet and covered him with the gun. Below the window, the procession was passing rather quickly, as I thought. I wished I could go up and look at it, but he was between the window and me and if he slept through it that would be the best arrangement possible. If he woke up, well, I had the gun with me at point-blank range. I would follow the method they used in films and command him not to stir until the procession passed. If he made the slightest movement, I would pull the trigger. My finger was on it already. Although I had had no practice with guns, I knew if I fiddled with the trigger the shot was bound to go off. I held the muzzle directly at his head, keeping it away, just out of his reach, in case he attempted to snatch (215).

Thus, Nataraj's *Sattva Guna* of compassion prevails throughout the novel. This trait is evident specially in his feeling for Kumar, the elephant who ultimately gets saved from the evil plans of Vasu.

In his novel, *The Vendor of Sweets*, Narayan showcases Jagan as being empathetic to other's needs. Jagan notices simple things, which might be causing discomfort to others. He arranges for a chair for 'one Mr Noble, an Englishman, the District Collector, who came for lessons in astrology and found it painful to sit on the floor and found it even more painful to extricate himself from the sitting posture at the end of the lessons' (11). He is concerned for "that little girl in the yellow skirt, ask her what she wants. She has been standing there so long!" (12). *Sattva Guna* shines in his compassionate personality when he says, "If everyone gave up dining leaves, those engaged in the leaf trade would be thrown out of their profession and an alternative engagement would have to be found for them" (16). He is in the business of making and selling sweets. Yet he is opposed to the idea of making profits by unfair means. He does 'not like the idea of cheating' (80) his customers and believes that 'it is purity that is important' (90). *Sattva Guna* of rationality, reason and compassion are further reflected in his personality when he says, "If others want to eat sweets, they must have the purest ones that is all. I am thinking particularly of children and poor people" (91). Jagan believes in the injunction: 'Perform thy charity without question' (83). Wisdom, compassion, kindness and his sense of duty are revealed in Jagan's persona in the following lines:

> "I work, because it's one's duty to work." He pulled the drawer, took out his Bhagvad Gita and read from it. "You see, it's my duty to go on doing something. Moreover"— he raised his voice — "that man and the other one and the one here, it supports them. What would our head cook do if it weren't for this establishment?" (40).

As a parent, Jagan is a kind father who is 'obsessed with his son's diet and brooded over the question night and day. At night before retiring, he held a long conference with his son on not only what he had eaten during the day but what he would prefer to eat the next day' (24-5). When he is about to lose his wife to a malignant tumour in her brain, 'the coarse, raw pain' (37) he feels for his son, Mali, remains embedded in some vital centre of his being. Later, when Mali goes into a shell and becomes detached, Jagan helps him, subtly, by leaving a five-rupee currency note on the hall table and checks 'later to find out if it had been accepted' (42). Mali makes plans of going to America without telling his father. When Jagan is informed about it by his cousin, Mali's safety is Jagan's prime concern. He says, "Please tell him to go by steamer. It's safer. Let him be safe. I don't like aeroplanes" (49).

Though the thoughts and actions of Jagan later show the dominance of *Rajas Guna* of attachment for his son, the *Sattva Guna* of selfless love for his daughter-in-law, Grace, makes him a man with qualities of kindness and compassion. Mali informs Jagan of his arrival and his accompanying woman. Jagan assumes her to be Mali's wife. Out of consideration for the new entrant to the house, Jagan spends a fortune in 'building a toilet and bathroom adjoining Mali's bedroom'. The walls are 'scrubbed and colour-washed…' (59). He appreciates Grace even though she is a foreigner and Mali has brought her home without his permission. He sees her as an individual and in his acceptance of her, starts 'getting used to the extreme air of orderliness that the feminine touch imparted to one's surroundings' (62). Jagan is soft in his words to her and says, "I didn't know much about you; even now I don't know much about you except that you are a good girl" (65). In fact, the generosity of his thoughts and actions surfaces when he believes and says, "We do not believe in caste nowadays.... Gandhi fought for its abolition" (66). In the end when he decides to leave his business and his house to be a 'free man' (184), he still thinks of helping Grace and tells the cousin, "If you meet her, tell her that if she ever wants to go back to her country, I will buy her a ticket. It's a duty we owe her. She was a good girl" (185).

Compassion and kindness are not possible without truth, which signifies another feature of the *Sattva Guna.* The man protagonist, Raman in *The Painter of Signs* shows compassion while speaking the truth (coupled with humour) towards his grandmother at the very beginning of the novel: 'On three occasions, you need not speak the truth. To save a life, to save an honour… and the third I can't remember, but I suppose to save an aunt the bother of cooking for you' (15). William Walsh writes:

> All that one can say for Raman is that this experience has helped him to achieve some measure of wry independence. No longer a child to be tended by his aunt, no more a lover and certainly not a husband, he does at least attain a degree of stability touched by disillusion (6).

At the same time, when Raman's aunt decides to go for a pilgrimage, he becomes 'very considerate and spends as much time as he could with her'. He feels 'he owed her at least his company' (163). He marvels 'at the simplicity of her life and her minimal wants' (165). Raman is compassionate towards his grandmother. He reflects:

Except the evening visit to the temple, her world was purely dedicated to his well-being. She had stayed at home, waiting to feed him, watching his moods to know if he was happy and contented. When he went out, she waited to open the door for him: when he spent all his evening with Daisy without coming home, she must have been in an agony (165).

When the grandmother instructs him with, "The milkman comes with the cow at four thirty in the morning. Someone must watch them, otherwise he will add water", Raman realises that if the 'curd and milk had been pure and creamy, it was only because she stood up beside the cow at dawn, peering into the milking pail'. He understands that he 'had taken so much for granted all these years! He was like a plant, tended with care, unaware of the continuous labour involved for the gardener. While he had been happily painting sign-boards or gossiping at The Boardless or gallivanting with Daisy, so much had been done backstage to keep him alive. It'd been a lifetime of dedication for another being, (165).

When Raman falls in love with the social worker, Daisy, his logical and reasoning mind (*Sattva Guna)*, associates it with the theory of love being 'blind' and that 'it probably also deadens the wits and makes one dumb. One likes to please the other at any cost' (63). When Raman tells his grandmother about Daisy, she is not very happy about it and says, "I have been hearing all sorts of stories. Did she run away from her parents?" Narayan takes the rhetoric thus:

> Raman overcame his irritation and replied, "It is nobody's business. She is a rare type of girl, devoted to the service of people and that is all her religion. I don't know if she cares for any other god or religion and I haven't asked. Her worship takes the form of service to the poor and the ignorant and helping them live a decent life. She cares not for wealth or luxury or titles. She can live with the poorest in their huts, eat their food and sleep on the mud floor… She is a good girl" (153).

Analysing the character of Raman, Nityananda Pattnayak writes:

> Narayan visualises Raman as a mythical figure who of all things said and hitherto done realises himself in the end as "A Painter of Signs and, and... what more shall I say?" or in Daisy's words, "an artist in lettering" (182), an artist whose art is sublime, who even at the moment of heightening physical desire "stroked her gently, letting his hand rest on her breasts; as he watched, her face wore a serenity he had not noticed before. Her angularities and self-assertiveness were gone. He was struck by the elegance of her form and features, suddenly saw her as an abstraction perhaps a goddess to be worshipped, not to be disturbed or defied with coarse fingers" (175). Thus, Raman experiences a kind of sublimity, for

whatever short duration it may be, in aesthetic body figure of his object of love. With him, the painting of signs remains from beginning to end a "mythical balance between active participation and acute withdrawal" (102).

In *A Tiger for Malgudi*, the Master is compassionate, considerate and tender towards the tiger. He does not regard the Tiger as a beast. When people at the circus are taking Raja away, he tells them:

> Keep him well. Remember he is only a tiger in appearance...He is a sensitive soul who understands life and its problems exactly as we do. Take him as a gift from God; only please don't put him in rough company. He is magnificent though he is not at his best now. After a few days of regular feeding at the zoo, he will get back the shine on his coat (175).

According to Michel Pousse, sincerity is always a prerequisite for success and it goes hand-in-hand with unselfishness. In *A Tiger for Malgudi,* Narayan spells it out distinctly. The tiger, man's arch enemy, has only known two masters. One, at the circus, who lives by the sword and so, logically meets his death at the tiger's claws. The second, The Master, speaks of love and thus makes a difference to the Tiger's life. In the only introduction Narayan has written to any of his novels he made his philosophy clear:

> Now in my story the 'tiger hermit' employs his powers to save the tiger and transform it inwardly working on the basis that, deep within, the core of personality is the same, in spite of differing appearances and categories and with the right approach you could expect the same response from a tiger as from any normal human being (65).

The Master's words are also full of compassion when he tells people to shun violence and destruction:

> If you are ready to hate and want to destroy each other, you may find a hundred reasons — a diversion of canal water in your field, two urchins of opposite camps slapping each other, rumours of molestation of some woman, even the right to worship in a temple, anything may spark off a fight if you are inclined to nurture hatred — only the foolish waste their lives in fighting (165).

The Master is kind and this gets cemented yet again when he talks to his wife of yesteryears. He converses with her because of his 'sympathies and a real desire to help' her, even though he is clear that he will 'never revive(s) the identity of the past in thought or word; its dead and buried' (172). K. Chellapan observes:

> In *A Tiger for Malgudi*, we find the theme of role playing and inner transformation in relation to a tiger whose straying out of its wilderness itself becomes a metaphor for a man losing his freedom by stepping out of the boundaries of his being. The tiger evolves into a symbol of God himself in his terrifying aspect and the Blakean link is unmistakable; but there is also the identity of the creator and the creature. Finally, it becomes a metaphor for man's fierceness as well as his ability to transcend his world as well as the body, both of which are prison houses at one level, but they themselves can be a means to transcend them. Here again, there is the disturbance of the equilibrium when the tiger becomes violent but finally it is made to accept its limitations. The tiger's search for freedom ends in its acceptance of its limitations, physical as well as environmental (ed. Srinath: 57).

Compassion signifies unselfish service to everyone. It entails forgiveness and understanding. The souls of these characters etched by Narayan are swayed by **Compassion**, thus marking their *Sattva Guna.*

Gandhian Way of Life

Gandhian Way of Life is synonymous with the *Sattva Guna* of truth and non-violence. Hence, the study of this particular characteristic adds a new dimension to the novels of Narayan. Gandhi practiced what he preached. He was disciplined in his food habits and meditation, practiced non-violence in thought and action while fighting for India's independence. He championed empathy for the poor and downtrodden, was in support of abolishing untouchability and advocated equality for women by promoting women's education. All these qualities show the presence of *Sattva Guna*. Since Narayan's men protagonists follow the teachings of Gandhi and tread the path shown by him, Gandhian way of life becomes synonymous with the *Sattva Guna.*

Elements of Gandhi's philosophy are rooted in the Indian religions of Jainism and Buddhism. Both of these advocate ahimsa (non-violence), which is "absence of the desire to kill or harm" (Chapple: 10). The *Acaranga Sutra*, a Jain text, describes the fundamental need for non-violence: "All beings are fond of life; they like pleasure and hate pain, shun destruction and like to live, they long to live. To all, life is dear" (Chapple: 11). Ahimsa is a way of living and thinking. Ravindra Kumar quotes Gandhi's words:

> Ahimsa cannot be dismissed as lightly as you think. Ahimsa is the strongest force known. But if all can use the strongest force with equal ease, it would lose its importance. We have not been able yet to discover the true measure of the innumerable properties of an article of our daily use like water. Some of its properties fill us with wonder. Let us not, therefore, make light of the strongest force like Ahimsa and let's try to discover its hidden power with patience and faith.

Karen Sihra, while studying the 'Philosophical Contributions of Gandhi's Ideas on Non-Violence' observes:

> Gandhi insists there are negative and positive elements of ahimsa. While his definition includes both elements, the distinction is important. The negative elements are defined as merely non-injury or absence of physical violence. The positive elements embrace much more than this. In its positive form, ahimsa means the largest love, the greatest charity. Ahimsa in its negative form involves only the individual. Love and charity are not extended when one refrains from injuring another, as love and charity are retained for the individual refraining from violence. Ahimsa in its purist and most positive form is a mental behaviour, a consciousness; therefore, the way one knows and carries out relationships is what is essentially important. In this form, ahimsa engages the other and extends oneself to the other. What results from this is peace with the other and a spiritual freedom for oneself (42-43).

Gandhian values, thoughts and his doctrine of love and ahimsa bear heavily on Narayan and it comes across in his writings in all his novels. At an individual level one can say that practically all of Narayan's heroes go through an 'experiment with truth'.Gandhi wanted to revive the spirit of Vivekananda and Ramakrishna to lift India out of the religious superstitions it had fallen into. Narayan's heroes prove to be very Gandhian in spirit (ed. C. N. Srinath: 63).

Digambar Singh Dewari who has analysed 'Gandhian Bearings on R. K. Narayan's Novels', maintains that 'Gandhi was essentially a man with a great sense of humour. Humour was not an additional gift to Gandhi. It was in the very blood that flowed in his veins. His subtle humour made him survive many personal and political crises' (105). Michel Pousse, whose research focuses on 'Narayan as a Gandhian Novelist' states that the theme developed by the Gandhian novelists are easily summed up because they are textbook applications of what the Mahatma ceaselessly repeated (61). All of Narayan's novels, from *Swami and Friends* (1935) to *Grandmother's Tale* (1992) bear the influence of Gandhian philosophy. However, *Waiting for the Mahatma* (1967) and *The Vendor of Sweets* (1967) bring out Gandhian underpinnings most strongly. Focusing on Gandhi's vision, as exhibited in the novels of Narayan, M. Sudha concludes that the principles of Gandhi are very well exhibited in Narayan's novels. Gandhi not only struggled for India's freedom, but also advocated non-violence. His 'Satyagraha' was based on boundless love and compassion. He spoke of truth and did not like falsehood:

> For example, in the novel *Waiting for the Mahatma*, Gandhiji himself has participated as a character. Bharti, an important personality in the novel serves as a disciple of Gandhiji....His novels serve as a panorama for the future generation, to know Gandhi as a whole (344).

In his novel *Waiting for the Mahatma* Narayan brings out the Gandhian philosophy and portrays Gandhi not only as a political leader, but also as a social thinker. Love blossoms between Sriram and Bharti with Gandhi being the backbone of the story. While highlighting the 'middle-period novels of R. K. Narayan', John Thieme claims that Sriram alternates between feelings of 'romantic importance, thinking he is a character out of an epic whose actions will determine future history and nostalgic longing for the tranquillity of his former Kabir Street life' (95). Slowly Sriram evolves as a human being because of the profound impact of Gandhian way of life on him. To Gandhi, truth is the eternal principle of life, the regulating force of the universe. It is synonymous to God and is the only path of discovery of self. Gandhian truth is explained by Bharti to Sriram:

> None except absolute truth-speakers are allowed to come into Mahatma's camp. People who come here must take an oath of absolute truth before going into Mahatma's presence (55).

Similarly, Gorpad, a volunteer in Gandhi's camp, says, "Mahatma will not let me be violent even in thought" (76). Further, while speaking to Sriram, Mahatma says, "(B)efore you aspire to drive the British from this country, you must drive every vestige of violence from your system. Remember that this is not going to be a fight with sticks and knives or guns but only with love" (77). Gandhian philosophy of 'Simple living, high thinking' is highlighted yet again in Bharti's words when she asks Sriram to sleep on the floor 'because Mahatmaji says so' (74). Mahatma's doctrine of selfless love is portrayed in Sriram's words, "Bapuji forbade us to refer to anyone in terms of religion as Muslims, Hindu, or Sikhs, but just as human beings" (244). Bharti's statement that "His (Gandhi's) last fast has completely fatigued him. Sometimes he lay there without moving, unconscious," (249), unearths Mahatma's belief of ahimsa and his strong will-power. Thus, Narayan, the master story teller that he is, brings out Gandhian philosophy of non-violence, love, truth, simple living high thinking in this novel. By making Mahatma a character in his story, he talks about Gandhi's love and respect for women, respect for all religions and castes and disgust at the practice of untouchability. Though the novel ends on a sad note of Gandhi's death, yet Narayan through his superb craftsmanship, leaves a message of hope. The reader is made to understand that Sriram and Bharti, after getting married, will work on Gandhian principles surely because their impending marriage has a seal of Mahatma's blessings.

Since the story in *The Man-Eater of Malgudi* is told in first person, we get to know of the *Sattva* qualities of the man protagonist, Nataraj from his own mouth, which have deep resonance with the Gandhian way of life. Waking up early every morning is depicted at the threshold of the novel. "My day started before four in the morning. The street would be quite dark when I set out to the river for my ablutions, except for the municipal lamps which flickered (if they had not run out of oil) here and there in our street. I went down Kabir street" (3*)*. Cold water bathing habit comes to the foray when he says, "At the touch of cold water around my body I felt elated. The trees on the bank stood like shadows in the dusk" (5). Further he is 'content to live' in the house as it had been left by his father (6). *Sattva Guna* of non-violence dominates his personality also because of his childhood value systems. Nataraj says:

> I had been brought up in a house where we were taught never to kill. When we swatted flies, we had to do it without the knowledge of our elders. I remember particularly one of my grand-uncles, who used the little room on the *pyol* and who gave me a coin every morning to buy sugar for the ants and kept an eye on me to see that I delivered the sugar to the ants in various corners of our house. He used to declare, with approval from all the others, "you must never scare away the crows and sparrows that come to share our food…" (65).

Non-violence and truth go together. Nataraj is seen to be influenced by the Mahatma's thoughts and does not argue just for the sake of an argument. In his own words:

> I suppressed the obvious repartees. Aggressive words only generate more aggressive words. Mahatma Gandhi had enjoined on us absolute non-violence in thought and speech, if for no better reason than to short-circuit violent speech and prevent it from propagating itself (70).

Even though Nataraj is disturbed by Vasu's aggressive behaviour and his mindless killing of animals, when asked, "It is true that he eats dogs?", "Oh, no," he says immediately and speaks the truth. "He eats rice and other stuff just as we do. That's all false" (103).

The Vendor of Sweets showcases Gandhi's values and philosophy through the character of the man protagonist Jagan. He wears "thick sandals made out of the leather of an animal which had died of old age". Being a follower of Gandhi, he explains, "I do not like to think that a living creature should have its throat cut for the comfort of my feet," and this occasionally involved him in excursions to remote villages where a cow or calf was reported to be dying (9). Jagan is satisfied with his profession of making and selling sweets. He has practically 'perfected the art of living on nothing' (10) and 'eats to live, that's all' (39). He is portrayed emulating Gandhi's philosophy of simple living and high thinking. He considers Gandhi to be his 'master' (106) and as a disciple has learnt not to 'nurse any resentment' (182). In tune with this, he does not accumulate or hoard wealth and allows it to grow naturally. He considers his business to be a service and therefore is not greedy for money. He says, "Money is an evil, we should all be happier without it. It is enough if an activity goes on self-supported; no need to earn money." (92). Further, Jagan is heard saying: "1937 — when Mahatma Gandhi had visited Malgudi and addressed a vast gathering on the sands of river. He spoke of service explaining how every human action acquired a meaning when it was performed as a service. Everyone should be free to serve humanity in his own way" (41). He again states at another place, "Well we don't believe in caste nowadays, you know," Jagan said generously; "Gandhi fought for its abolition" (66). To follow Gandhi's footsteps, Jagan wears khadi and spins charkha:

> The slight whirring noise of wheel and the thread growing out of it between one's thumb and forefinger were very comforting, stilling the nerves and thought. Gandhi had prescribed spinning for the economic ills of the country, but also for any deep agitation of the mind (121).

At the end of the story when Jagan decides to leave his business and the city, he is determined to "seek a new interest – different from the set of repetitions performed for sixty years. I am going somewhere; not carrying more than what my shoulder can bear" (183). Among other things in his little bundle is a charkha because "It's a duty I owe Mahatma Gandhi, I made a vow before him that I would spin everyday of my life. I've got to do it, whether I'm at home or in a forest" (176).

Raman, in *The Painter of Signs*, is influenced by Gandhi's wisdom. He is seen reflecting on his words:

> Mahatma Gandhi had advised "walk with your eyes fixed on your toes during the day and on the stars at night." He would be saved if she did not flash her eyes on him and he would follow Mahatma Gandhi's formula and look at the ground while talking. The eye was really the source of mischief. One's thoughts followed what

the eye saw. Thoughts developed from sight. He would wear coloured glasses so that she might not note where he was looking (40).

This novel also portrays Narayan's skill of viewing a woman as an individual. Through the man protagonist, Raman, he makes the reader realise that Daisy could be right in her choice of a career over marriage and thus never complained about any discomforts or hardships associated with her work. Narayan gives the *Sattva Guna* of altruism and empathy to Sriram for him to realise the 'difference of opinion' in Daisy's personality.

Gandhian way of life advocates contentment and patience. Thus, The Master's words in *A Tiger for Malgudi* are in sync with Gandhi's philosophy. He says:

> Do not crave for the unattainable. It's enough you have realisation. All in good time. We cannot understand God's intentions. All growth takes place in its own time. If you brood on your improvements rather than your shortcomings, you will be happier. In short you don't have to know the business of counting, which habit has made us human beings miserable in many ways. We have lost the faculty of appreciating the present living moment. We are always looking forward or backward and waiting for one or sighing for the other and lose the pleasure of awareness of the moment in which we actually exist (160-1).

Sattva Guna of non-violence gets underlined further when The Master defines, "All causes of rivalry and clash" are senseless and so do not need "defining or explanation". He advises people never to fight for "no cause is worth a clash" (165). Gandhian path is extremely prominent in Narayan's novels and many of the characters **follow the Gandhian Way of Life**. The way in which they imbibe it, along with practices of non-violence, makes this an outstanding *Sattva Guna* in their personality.

Religious Bent of Mind and Spirituality

Religious Bent of Mind and Spirituality is a quality which can be researched under the *Sattva Guna* because the word religion is often used interchangeably with faith, belief system or set of duties.

Spirituality is defined as a process of personal transformation in accordance with religious ideals and emphasises humanistic ideas on moral qualities such as love, compassion, patience, tolerance, forgiveness, contentment, responsibility, harmony and a concern for others. A religion is an organised collection of beliefs, cultural systems and world-views that relate humanity to an order of existence. Many religions have narratives, symbols and sacred histories that are intended to explain the meaning of life and/or to explain the origin of life or the Universe. From their beliefs about the cosmos and human nature, people derive morality, ethics, religious laws or a preferred lifestyle. Many religions may have organised behaviours, clergy, a definition of what constitutes adherence or membership, holy places and scriptures. The practice of a religion may also include rituals, sermons, commemoration or veneration of a deity, gods or goddesses, sacrifices, festivals, feasts, trance, initiations, funerary services, matrimonial services, meditation, prayer, music, art, dance, public service or other aspects of human culture. Religions may also contain mythology.

The typical dictionary definition of religion refers to a 'belief in, or the worship of, a God or Gods' or the 'service and worship of God or the supernatural'. However, writers and scholars have expanded upon the 'belief in God' definitions as insufficient to capture the diversity of religious thought and experience. Indian religions are sometimes classified as the *dharmic religions*, as they all feature dharma, the specific law of reality and duties expected according to the religion. Concepts most of them share in common include *karma*, caste, reincarnation, *mantras*, *yantras* and *darshana*. Hinduism is the most ancient of still-active religions, with origins perhaps as far back as prehistoric times. Hinduism is not a monolithic religion but a religious category containing dozens of separate philosophies amalgamated as *Sanâtana Dharma,* which is the name with which Hinduism has been known throughout history by its followers. Since the nineteenth century spirituality is often separated from religion and has become more oriented on subjective experience and psychological growth. It may refer to almost any kind of meaningful activity or blissful experience, but without a single, widely-agreed definition. Not all modern notions of spirituality embrace transcendental ideas.

P. S. Sundaram observes Narayan's novels as 'religious fables'. *Waiting for the Mahatma* and *The Vendor of Sweets* bear significantly on Gandhian view of religion. In *Waiting for the Mahatma* a huge gathering awaiting the arrival of the fictional Gandhi are engrossed in chanting 'Raghupati Raghav Raja Ram, Pathitha Pavana Seetha Ram'. In his public address Gandhi calls upon the audience to chant 'Ram Dhun', do 'spinning on the chakra' and to follow 'the practice of absolute truth and non-violence'. Thereafter, he advises Sriram to spin, read the *Bhagvad Gita* and utter *Ram nam* continuously. Later Gandhi conveys to Bharti, through his letter, how he wished that she could read Tulsi Das' Ramayana without any assistance. He further adds: "Wherever you may be with a copy of Ramayan and Gita and a spinning wheel, there you are rightly occupied" (51). Gandhi describes his faith in God:

> I am surer of His existence than of the fact that you and I sitting in the room. Then, I can also testify that I may live without air and water but cannot live without him. You can pluck out my eyes but that cannot kill me. But blast my belief in God and I am dead (61).

Dewari states:

> Narayan's novels manifest this Gandhian faith in God through various ways - prayers, pilgrimages, religious discourses, references to scriptures and the characters figuring in them, preponderance of the temple of various deities, the scriptural echo in the naming of the major characters (52).

In *The Man-Eater of Malgudi*, there exists a deep mythical structure. The story of the peaceful printer Nataraj who must overcome the demon like Vasu is structured very much like a myth. As myths and spirituality are implicit in Hindu society, the world of Malgudi is full of mythical elements. To complement these mythical elements, comparisons and references are made to various Hindu myths throughout the book. These act as signposts to the significance of what is going on in the story itself. The battle between Vasu and Nataraj is framed perfectly in the context of myth. The action that occurs in the novel bears many similarities to other myths that are mentioned, in the *Ramayana* and the myth of *Bhasmasura*. The structure of the story is the same as a myth, with the protagonist facing an enemy who eventually meets his end by his own hand. Ashok Kumar Kundu analyses:

> Narayan draws directly from the myths of our epics and classics. By using them successfully in metaphor, personification and symbol, he has kept tradition alive. Through his writings, Narayan has expressed his world view. His writing shows that he believes in eternity, karma and the theory of reincarnation. He seems to consider emancipation from the wheel of the life as the pinnacle of human desire. Moreover, his interpretation of life is spiritualistic (147).
>
> Myths we know are not merely fanciful stories but pragmatic embodiments of moral wisdom and primitive faith. They are a medium of moral instruction and myth makers are great philosophers and teachers. Myths not only set exemplary patterns of behaviour but set the scale of values as well as the ideal goals. Human being emulates the behaviour of divine beings or their mythical ancestors. Myths can therefore be said to have a power to change a man's life (148).

The protagonist, Nataraj is shown to bear traits with the predominant *Sattva Guna*. Vasu's profession of taxidermy provides a direct challenge to Nataraj's belief in the sanctity of life and this is underscored by various mythological references. When Nataraj visits Vasu's attic, he is shocked to discover the carcasses of various animals including a cat that has frequented his press, a tiger poached from the forest and a stuffed crow. Seeing the room full of carcasses of animals, with blood and stench all over, he can't 'imagine any human being living in this atmosphere' (60). He is aghast when he notices that Vasu has killed a crow and asks him, "What did the crow do to you?" (62). The full extent of his repugnance come forth when he realises that it is the sacred 'garuda' (63). Nataraj says and ponders on the situation thus:

> "Don't you realise that it's sacred? That it's the messenger of God Vishnu?" I shivered slightly at the thought and the way his mind worked. Nothing seemed to touch him. No creature was safe, if it had the misfortune to catch his eye. I had made a mistake in entertaining him. I ought to send him away at the earliest possible

> moment. His presence defiled my precincts. My mind seethed with ideas as to how to throw him out, but he noticed nothing (64).

Religion and the rituals of worship associated with it, come on board when Narayan describes the temple, ceremonies and the statue of God in detail:

> The God was beautifully decorated. He wore a rose garland and a diamond pendant sparkled on his chest. He had been draped in silk and gold lace and he held a flute in his hand: and his little bride, a golden image draped in blue silk and sparkling with diamonds, was at his side, the shy bride. The piper was blowing his cheeks out, filling the air with "Kalyani Rag", a lovely melody at this hour. The temple was nearly a century old, built by public subscription in the days when my grandfather and a few others had come here as pioneers (178-9).

One of Nataraj's friends is a poet, who is writing an epic about the life of Krishna, an incarnation of Vishnu and during the course of action the poet arrives at the moment of the hero's marriage to Radha. To celebrate this event, it is agreed to hold an elaborate ceremony, centred on an elephant in conjunction with the annual spring festival at the local Krishna temple. Worried that Vasu, who has been quick to grasp the commercial possibilities of a dead elephant, will try to kill it, Nataraj initially feels that he must act as an elephant's protector, but then remembers a mythic tale that suggests otherwise:

> The sight of the God, the sound of music, the rhythm of cymbals and the scent of jasmine and incense induced in me a temporary indifference to everything. Elephant? Who could kill an elephant? There came to my mind the tale of elephant Gajendra, the elephant of mythology who stepped into a lake and had his leg caught in the jaws of a mighty crocodile; and the elephant trumpeted helplessly, struggled and in the end desperately called on Vishnu, who immediately appeared and gave him the strength to come ashore out of the jaws of a crocodile. In this story I told myself, "Our ancestors have shown us that an elephant has a protected life and no one can harm it." I felt lighter at heart. When the time came the elephant would find the needed strength. The priest was circling the camphor light before the golden images

> and the reflections on the faces made them vibrate with a living quality. God Krishna was really an incarnation of Vishnu, who had saved Gajendra; he would again come to the rescue of the same animal (180).

The novel is full of words of wisdom and knowledge coupled with faith and spirituality. Sastri tells the man protagonist Nataraj that 'Every man can think that he is great and will live forever, but no one can guess from which quarter his doom will come' (95) and at the end of the novel that '(E)very demon appears in the world with a special boon of indestructibility. Yet the universe has survived all the *rakshasas* that were ever born. Every demon carries within him, unknown to himself, a tiny seed of self-destruction and goes up in thin air at the most unexpected moment. Otherwise what is to happen to humanity?' (240).

Sattva Guna of spirituality and religious belief also means eating pure food like vegetables, milk products, pulses and grains, which are generally good for us. It also implies consuming food items only for one's need. Further, the correct time for eating meals is also outlined in holy scriptures. Thus, Jagan, the man protagonist in *The Vendor of Sweets* is outraged when his son Mali writes to him that he has taken to eating beef. Jagan in his understanding of shastras knows that 'killing of a cow' headed the list of five deadly sins (56-7). Jagan has moderate eating and drinking habits. He does not 'drink more than four ounces of water a day' which is 'boiled at night and cooled in a mud jug open to the sky' (103) and 'keeps off sweets and salt' (114). In fact, he firmly believes that 'diet has a lot to do with the colour of one's hair' (107). Throughout the story, Narayan lets the readers know of Jagan's plans of writing a book on 'diet controlled according to nature's specifications' (108).

Tabish Khair points out that it is a mistake to see Narayan's characters as aspirants of 'spiritual maturity'. Instead, they aspire for 'Existential maturity'. In Khair's view, a significant number of Narayan's protagonists are not very spiritual or religious. They are primarily concerned with the secular problem of living, though they often mechanically observe religious customs. (Thieme:126)

Religion and spirituality also entail a deep connection with nature. The men protagonists of Narayan often reveal this aspect.

In *The Vendor of Sweets,* Jagan remembers his 'father who died at ninety without a single tooth loose in his jaw'. Jagan has immense faith in the properties of margosa and in spite of it bitterness, he calls it 'amrita', the ambrosia which kept the God alive; and sometimes he calls it 'sanjeevani' the rare herb mentioned in the epics which, when, held at the nostrils, could bring the dead to life. Jagan stresses being as close to nature as possible. According to him, 'Socks should never be worn because they are certain to heat the blood through interference with the natural radiation which occurs through one's soles and also because you insulate yourself against beneficial magnetic charges of the earth's surface' (68).

Hindu religious scriptures state a wife's place as next to her husband. Jagan believes in this philosophy. When Mali informs him that his 'wife' Grace will go back to her own country if she has no work, Jagan's view, "But a wife must be with her husband, whatever happens", says it all about his religious bent of mind. Similarly, as a husband he is aware of his own duties towards his wife and his faith that husband and wife should be together at all times is highlighted when he says, "Use or no use, my wife.... I look after her all her life" (135). Jagan is upset when he finally comes to know that Grace and Mali are not married and are living together in his house. This is a blow to his strong sense of righteousness and religious beliefs. *Sattva Guna* of celibacy is worded by Jagan when he says:

> Nature has never meant sex to be anything more than a means of propagation of the species, that one drop of white blood was equal to forty drops of red blood and that seminal waste and nervous exhaustion reduced one's longevity, the essence of all achievement being celibacy and conservation (166).

Divinity and purity dominate his thoughts. He keeps a copy of *Bhagvad Gita*, refers to it as "truly a treasure-house of wisdom" and reads it everyday. He believes that there is no such thing as reading this book finally; it is something to be read all one's life. He quotes Lord Krishna in the *Gita*, "It is all in one's hand. You make up your mind and you will find object of your search," and that, "The Gita also says every man must perform his duty in the right spirit and right measure" (99-100). R. K. Narayan talks of the ultimate truth of life in the dialogue he gives the male protagonist, "The world doesn't collapse even when a great figure is assassinated or dies of heart failure. Think that my heart has failed, that's all" (184).

In *A Painter of Signs*, Raman is under the guardianship of his grandmother, whose father, 'was a priest and officiated at birthdays, funerals and all kinds of religious functions and brought home his fee in the form of rice and vegetables and coconut and sugarcane'. Thus, Raman, at an early age, is exposed to grandmother's version of religion and customs. She informs Raman that 'a cow when gifted to a Brahmin' helped a 'dead man's soul to ford a difficult river in the next world' (19). Raman who propagates rationality asks 'how?', to which his grandmother replies, "That's what our shastras say and we don't have to question it. It is the duty of the living to help the dead with proper rituals" (19). Raman sometimes believes in the philosophy: 'Man must live for the moment and extract its essence. Every minute becomes a yesterday and is lost forever. Today is tomorrow's yesterday' (93). Thus, he chooses to act on it to satisfy the pleasure of the flesh. However, he has an answer for his behaviour for he knows that 'people are moved by strange inexplicable drives' (64). In this novel too, Narayan has subtly touched upon the story of *Santanu,* a legend from *Mahabharata.* The relationship between Raman and Daisy is based on *King Santanu* and goddess *Ganga.*

In *A Tiger for Malgudi*, the following excerpt clearly shows Narayan's strong bent of spirituality and his belief in karmic accounts. His theory of 'as you sow, so shall you reap' is an age-old dictate of Hindu philosophy:

> Bars of iron, unbending and perpetually pressing against one's face. I had had no contact with any sort of metal in my life; now this combination of man and metal subdued me – metal which in various forms served the evil ends of man as prison bars, traps and weapons. I desperately tried to smash the bars again and again and only made my head bloody (47).
>
> Later, when I explained this stage of my life to my Master, he said, "You probably in a previous life enjoyed putting your fellow-beings behind bars. One has to face the reaction of every act, if not in the same life, at least in another life or series of lives. There

can be no escape from it. Now you have a chance to realise how your prisoners must have felt in those days, when you locked them in and watched them day by day to measure how far you had succeeded in breaking their spirits."

"Why should I have done that?"

"I can't answer it; people only follow their inclinations and sooner or later their reward or retribution. That's the natural law of life, as inevitable as the ripening of a mango in its season or the fall of a withered leaf" (48).

Ashok Kumar Kundu states:

The dim beginning of the awakening of soul of his protagonists in his earlier novels culminates in his protagonist's rising to the higher state of Vedantic awareness in *A Tiger for Malgudi.* Malgudi is an imaginary town but it has been drawn with such conviction that some people have even drawn the map of the town with its landmark. The topography around Malgudi and its architectural setting in terms of crowded streets, the bazars and public places like the railway station, the schools, the colleges, etc., are recurrent vicinities in his novels. Although the impact of modernity changes its inhabitants outwardly yet at some point of their life, they are unable to resist the pull of ancient metaphysical India. At this juncture of life, the protagonists of his novels understand the value of leading life based on traditional value and religion (70).

Further, Narayan's explanation of death is:

Life or death is in no one's hands; you can't die by willing or escape death by determination. A great power has determined the number of breaths for each individual, who can neither stop them nor prolong...That's why God says in the *Gita,* "I am life and death, I'm the killer and the killed...Those enemies you see before you, O Arjuna, are already dead, whether you aim your arrows at them or not!" (142).

Lakshmi Holmstrom indicates that development of Narayan's protagonists is related to the four *asramas* (or stages) in the ideal Hindu life. Narayan's fiction is underpinned by these four stages, respectively known as the *brahmacharya, grihastya, vanaprastha* (the 'shadowy' third stage in which the householder becomes a forest-dweller or hermit prior to the final renunciation) and *sanyasa* (Thieme: 12-3). Hindu ways of living, the four *asramas*, are subtly discussed here. The maturity of thought as one grows, learning to control words, temper, greed and lust with ripening of age has been portrayed by Narayan yet again in *A Tiger for Malgudi*:

> It's a natural condition of existence. Every creature is born with a potential store of violence. A child, even before learning to walk, with a pat of its chubby hands just crushes the life out of a tiny ant crawling near it. And as he grows all through life he maintains a vast store of aggressiveness, which will be subdued if he is civilised, or expended in some manner that brings retaliation. But violence cannot be everlasting. Sooner or later, it has to go, if not through wisdom, definitely through decrepitude, which comes on with years, whether one wants it or not. The demon, the tormentor, or the tyrant in history, if he ever survives to experience senility, becomes helpless and dependent, lacking the strength even to swat a fly. You are now an adult, full-grown tiger and assuming you are fifteen years old, in human terms you would be over seventy years old and at seventy and onwards one's temper gets toned down through normal decay and let us be grateful for it. You cannot continue your ferocity forever. You have to change... (145).

The Master describes God as 'The creator, the great spirit pervading every creature, every rock and tree and the stars, a source of power and strength' (157-8). He sees the tiger as a life form having 'only the appearance of a tiger, but he is not one-inside he is no different from you and me' (145-6). The Master echoes the age-old wisdom in steadying one's mind:

> This is one of the rules of yoga to steady one's mind, to look down one's nose and at nothing beyond. That's one way not to be distracted and to maintain one's peace of mind. I would ask you to keep your head bowed and cast your eyes down and make no sort of sound, whatever may be the reaction of the people we pass (149).

He believes that 'The eye is the starting point of all evil and mischief. The eye can travel far and pick out objects indiscriminately, mind follows the eye and rest of the body is conditioned by the mind. Thus, starts a chain of activity which may lead to trouble and complication, or waste of time if nothing else' (155). He acknowledges the presence of God in details and describes it 'in his own terms as the Creator, the Great Spirit pervading every creature, every rock and tree and the sky and the stars; a source of power and strength.... What we must not forget is that He may be everything we imagine and more' (156). The *Gita* gets quoted yet again when he says, "In *Bhagvad Gita* He reveals himself in a mighty terrifying form which pervades the whole universe in every form of life and action. Remember also He is within every one of us and we derive our strength from Him" (158).

The company one keeps directly impacts the thought, words and actions. The value of *satsang* has been highly emphasised in Hinduism. The presence of people with right beliefs and thoughts has a power to change us for the better. Similarly, *kusang* can also influence us towards falsehood, greed, anger, jealousy and delusion. The Master's presence in Raja's life brings metamorphosis in him. The Master does not treat Raja as an animal. Raja feels grateful that the master is trying to transform him in so many ways. That there is a worth of every stage of life, a significance of all we do, is highlighted under the *Sattva Guna* by the Master when he says:

> You may get in now, Raja, a new life opens before you. Men, women and children, particularly children, hundreds of them will come to see you. You will make them happy (176).

Narayan closes the novel illustrating his strong view and belief in the theory of reincarnation. Raja's going away from The Master is certainly not the end for "Both of us will shed our forms soon and perhaps we could meet again, who knows? So goodbye for the present" (176).

All the above characters have a very strong bearing of **Spirituality and Religious bent of Mind** shaping their personalities under the impact of *Sattva Guna.*

Hence, it can be said that men protagonists of Narayan, discussed in this chapter viz. **Sriram** in *Waiting for the Mahatma,* **Nataraj** in *The Man-Eater of Malgudi,* **Jagan** in *The Vendor of Sweets,* **Raman** in *The Painter of Signs* and **The Master** in *A Tiger for Malgudi* embody various characteristics of *Sattva Guna*. They are epitomes of positive values and virtues, which combined with the Gandhian values and essence of Hinduism, give each of them a rare depth. Seeing their characteristics under the rubric of *Sattva Guna* is fruitful, as it encompasses a multitude of 'positive', 'good' and 'life-defining' traits.

3

Impact of *Rajas Guna*

Novels and Characters

Narayan expresses in his novels the Indian ethos. Though he writes in English language, he writes of India, Indian culture, Indian people, Indian family and Hindu Mythology. He talks of the economic, social and religious life in India. Malgudi, the fictional town where Narayan bases his novels, has been called the microcosm of India. Ethos, intrinsically Indian, is expressed in his characters through their respective attachment in relationships in joint family system, rituals, customs and traditions. R.K. Narayan's view of social amalgamation is Indian and therefore his characters are involved in occupations primarily as school-teachers, poets, printers, householders, money-vendors or office-goers.

Graham Greene's oft quoted comment 'without him I could never have known what it is like to be an Indian' is the most famous of many testimonials to Narayan's supposed grasp of essential Indianness. C.D. Narsimhaiah, who, despite a preference for Narayan's contemporary, Raja Rao, says of him, 'Few writers have been more truly Indian'. Three of Narayan's initial novels – *Swami and Friends*, *The Bachelors of Arts* and *The English Teacher* are often grouped together as a trilogy about the evolving man protagonist, a figure whose name changes from novel to novel, but whose relationships and situations as a young Brahmin, experiencing various stages of the English-oriented colonial educational curriculum and gradually making the transition from the first to the second of the four *ashramas* of the Manusmriti remains constant.

The portrayal of characters within the framework of the four *ashramas* combined with intrinsic Hindu values and ethos impacts the men protagonists in such a way that there is predominance of *Rajas Guna.* The influence of desire, passion, power, obedience, attachment, action and energy engulfs many men protagonists.

As described in *Bhagvad Gita,* chapter 14*:*

"RAJAS is passion. Rajas is desire. Rajas is unlit activity. It leads to unrest and strife. Rajas binds the body to action. Rajas stays either with stark dynamism or with blind aggression. Restlessness and Rajas breathe together. To separate toil from Rajas is practically impossible. Rajas is another name for passionate movement. If one dies when Rajas prevails, then he is reborn among those attached to action".

Narayan in his novels ***Swami and Friends* (1935), *The Bachelor of Arts* (1937), *The English Teacher* (1945), *Mr. Sampath* (1949), *The Guide* (1956) and *The Talkative Man* (1986)** carves out men protagonists in a storyline where the *Rajas Guna* is predominant.

Swaminathan in *Swami and Friend,*

Chandran in *The Bachelor of Arts*

Krishna in *The English Teacher*

Sampath in *Mr. Sampath*

Raju in *The Guide*

Madhu in *A Talkative Man* are men protagonists who show qualities of action, restlessness, ambition, desire, obedience and passion. These men have an ambition to succeed, often get restless with what they are doing, are passionate about relationships, wish to please their elders and are full of energy. They believe in doing their duty in sync with the pleasures of the flesh. Thus, they show predominance of *Rajas Guna.* To study and understand the impact of *Rajas Guna* on the men protagonists in Narayan's novels, the chief four characteristics prevalent under this *Guna* are undertaken. They are

(a) Desire, Passion and Lust

(b) Attachment

(c) Obedience

(d) Ambition and Action.

Narayan's novel, *Swami and Friends* (1935), narrates the life of the protagonist, Swaminathan, through his own eyes. It is a simple story of Swami, a charming boy who lives in a world of assertive parents and strict teachers. He is a student at a British – established mission school who does what most students of his age do viz. dodge homework, find ways to cope up with teachers and parents, play cricket with friends, try to impress peers and many a times act on impulse. His friendship with Rajam, the son of a police officer and the captain of the cricket team is instrumental in highlighting his emotional psyche. As unrest threatens India and Swami navigates through a series of misadventures, he learns to act like a man. He manages his tough balancing act for a while but then two incidents change his life forever. Finally, he gets out of trouble, but the cost is heavy: he loses the friendship of Rajam and is devastated at his departure at the end.

The novel describes the rainbow world of childhood and addresses the pleasures and pains in the journey of 'growing up'. Narayan's personal experience at school has gone into the making of this novel. Swami easily fits into the impact of predominating *Rajas Guna* primarily because of his young age which is marked by impulsiveness, restlessness, action and non-conformity.

*The Bachelor of Arts (*1937) is also set in the fictional town Malgudi. The story explores the transition of an adolescent, Chandran, into adulthood. The novel begins with Chandran's college life. After graduation, he falls in love with a girl, the marriage proposal is rejected by the bride's parents, since his horoscope describes him as a *manglik*. Frustrated and desperate, he embarks on a journey of a Sanyasi where he meets many people. He gets misunderstood as a great sage by some villagers. Due to the compunctions and realisations, he decides to return home. He takes up a job as a news agent and decides to marry. This he does to please his parents, thinking of the discomfort he had caused them earlier. The man protagonist fits perfectly in *Rajas Guna* because his personality leans towards attachment, unrest and action. Through the course of the novel, Chandran is seen as a restless individual, yet to find an identity or self-awareness. His brief stint as a sanyasi is more because of a temporary loss of confidence in himself and due to dejection at having lost his love interest rather than due to rising above the pleasures of the flesh. Thus, his character is fit to be studied under the predominating *Rajas Guna.*

The English Teacher (1945) is dedicated to Narayan's wife Rajam. It has not only an autobiographical element but is poignant in its intensity of feeling. The story is a series of experiences in the life of Krishna, an English teacher and his quest towards achieving inner peace and self-development. As an English teacher at Albert Mission College, Krishna leads a mundane and monotonous lifestyle, but this takes a turn when his wife, Susila and their child, Leela, come to live with him. He realises his life is more complete with family around and that it is not limited to teaching in the college. Krishna wishes to make a 'home' and takes Susila along to look for a suitable house. However, Susila contracts typhoid after visiting a dirty lavatory, keeping her in bed for weeks. Throughout the entire course of her illness, Krishna constantly tries to keep an optimistic view about Susila's ailment, but Susila eventually succumbs to her sickness and passes away. Krishna, destroyed by her loss, has suicidal thoughts but gives them up for the sake of his daughter, Leela. Soon after, he receives a letter from a stranger who indicates that the spirit of Susila has been in contact with him and that she wants to communicate with Krishna. This leads to Krishna's journey in search of enlightenment. Leela, on the other hand, goes to a preschool where Krishna gets to meet the caring Headmaster. The Headmaster's priority is his school and the students. However, he decides to leave the school on a day predicted by an astrologer to be his 'dying day'. This prophecy does not come true. An eye-opener for Krishna, he eventually learns to communicate with Susila on his own with 'rare immutable joy' (184). Krishna, the man protagonist in this novel shows the impact of *Rajas Guna* due to extreme attachment to his wife and child. All the actions of Krishna throughout the story carry this main trait of *Rajas Guna*, be it in his actions, words or thoughts.

Mr. Sampath (1949) ranks very high in the world of Indo-Anglian fiction. The novel is the story of Srinivas and the printer, Mr. Sampath. Srinivas comes to Malgudi looking for someone who would print his journal, *The Banner*. He is introduced to Mr. Sampath. Mr. Sampath starts printing *The Banner*. When the publication is suspended due to a strike in the press, Mr. Sampath decides to turn a film producer. He sets up the *Sunrise Picture Studio* and offers Srinivas the job of a script -writer. The *Rajas Guna* of restlessness, activity and ambition dominates the personality of Mr. Sampath. He decides to produce the film titled *The Burning of Kama* and takes up the role of *Shiva*. Attraction and lust for the heroine, Shanti is yet another trait which impacts Mr. Sampath's persona. The story progresses and soon the film-producing venture also comes to an end. Srinivasa is upset, severs all connections with the film world and revives the publication of *The Banner*.

In the end, Mr. Sampath leaves Malgudi to escape the notice of his creditors. He bears all the traits of *Rajas Guna.* He is ambitious and active. He wants to achieve success and money. Besides, lust, passion and attraction to the woman protagonist, cements his personality under the *Rajas Guna.*

The Guide (1956) is the most popular novel of R.K. Narayan. It also won him the Sahitya Academy Award. Narayan narrates the adventures of a tourist guide, 'Raju'. This vocation introduces Raju to Marco and his beautiful wife, Rosie. While the husband is busy with work as an archaeologist, Raju and Rosie get into a relationship. Ultimately the husband comes to know of their affair and goes away to Madras. Rosie comes to stay with Raju. She is a dancer and Raju helps her perform in public. Soon she gets popular and this increases their earnings tremendously. Raju lives lavishly, entertains a large number of friends with whom he drinks and gambles. All goes well till Raju forges Rosie's signatures to obtain her valuable jewellery. The act lands him in jail. Rosie leaves Malgudi and goes away to Madras, her home-town. She pursues her dancing and does well even without Raju's help. On his release from jail, Raju takes shelter in a deserted temple on the banks of river, Sarayu. The villagers nearby take him to be a Mahatma and begin to worship him. Raju is quite comfortable and performs the new role of a saint to perfection. However, a severe famine and drought engulfs the village. Turn of events make the villagers believe that Raju has undertaken a fast to bring in the rains. Despite his best efforts to the contrary, he has to undertake the fast. The fast attracts much attention and people come to have *darshan* of the Mahatma from far and wide. On the twelfth day of the fast, Raju falls down exhausted just as there are signs of rain on the distant horizon.

Raju, the protagonist in the novel, shows all sovereign characteristics of the *Rajas Guna*. Desire and passion for another man's wife, greed for money, ambition to get more and more, cheating by forgery and pretending to be a sanyasi to gain power on villagers, are traits of *Rajas Guna* in Raju's personality deftly carved by the master story-teller R.K. Narayan.

*Talkative Man (*1986) by R.K. Narayan is also set in the fictional town of Malgudi. In this novel, Narayan entertains with the central characters of Dr Rann and that of the Talkative Man. The man protagonist, Madhu has all the highlighting characteristics of *Rajas Guna*. In fact, the very name 'Talkative Man' is apt to study him under the impacting *Rajas Guna.* A talkative man is restless, active and many a times speaks for no reason.

Thus, all the six, above mentioned, men protagonists of Narayan show the qualities of *Rajas Guna*. The research of the chief characteristics of this *Guna,* one at a time and its impact on the men protagonists gives Narayan's novels a new perspective.

Desire, Passion and Lust

When Desire, Passion and Lust impact the men protagonists, *Rajas Guna* reigns supreme. Desire is a sense of longing or hoping for a person, object or outcome. When a person desires something or someone, the sense of longing is excited by the enjoyment or the thought of the item or person, thus leading to actions to obtain the goal. The motivational aspect of desire has long been noted by philosophers. Thomas Hobbes (1588–1679) asserted that human desire is the fundamental motivation of all human action. Desire can cause humans to become obsessed and embittered. It has been called one of the causes of woe for mankind. Within the teachings of Buddhism, desire is thought to be the cause of all suffering that one experiences in human existence. The eradication of desire or craving leads to rising above the three *Gunas* and ultimate happiness (*Nirvana*).

Passion means strong emotion, intense sexual love and extreme enthusiasm for something. Lust is an emotion or feeling of intense desire in the body. Lust manifests in many forms such as the lust for knowledge, the lust for carnal desires or the lust for power. It can take such mundane forms as lust for food which is distinct from the need for food. Lust is a powerful psychological force producing intense wanting for an object, or circumstances fulfilling the emotion. Lust is the clinging to, attachment to, identification with and passionate desire for certain things in existence. Thus, lust is the ultimate cause of general imperfection and the most immediate root cause of suffering.

In the *Bhagvad Gita,* Lord Krishna, an Avatar of Vishnu declares that lust is one of the gates to *Naraka* or hell. States *Bhagavd Gita:*

> Arjuna said: 'O descendant of Vrsni, by what is one impelled to sinful acts, even unwillingly, as if engaged by force'? Then Krishna said: 'It is lust only, Arjuna, which is born of contact with the material mode of passion and later transformed into wrath and which is the all-devouring sinful enemy of this world. As fire is covered by smoke, as a mirror is covered by dust, or as the embryo is covered by the womb, the living entity is similarly covered by different degrees of this lust. Thus, the wise living entity's pure consciousness becomes covered by his eternal enemy in the form of lust, which is never satisfied and which burns like fire. The senses, the mind and the intelligence are the sitting places of this lust. Through them lust covers the real knowledge of the living entity and bewilders him. Therefore, O Arjuna, best of the Bharatas, in the very beginning curb this great symbol of sin—(lust) by regulating the senses and slay this destroyer of knowledge and self-realisation. The working senses are superior to dull matter; mind is higher than the senses; intelligence is still higher than the mind; and he [the soul] is even higher than the intelligence. Thus, knowing oneself to be transcendental to the material senses, mind and intelligence, O mighty-armed Arjuna, one should steady the mind by deliberate spiritual intelligence and thus—by spiritual strength—conquer this insatiable enemy known as lust (*Bhagvad Gita*).

In Narayan's first novel *Swami and Friends* a definite thematic pattern is traced. It is termed as a desire for quest of identity and maturity. When the novel opens, Swaminathan is a mere child.

He undergoes a number of experiences resulting in psychological changes and growth. The novel has shades of Narayan's autobiography. It owes much of its realism and authenticity to the fact that it is rooted in Narayan's personal experience as a boy at school. It is a time of life when the colours of the world are different and a natural state of joy prevails over simple things in life. The fact that Narayan chooses to pen down his own experiences underlines his desire to address his emotions and to resolve them. The passion for his writings also gets highlighted in the nature of the characters he chooses as protagonists. This, in itself has traits of *Rajas Guna* which invariably comes out in most of his novels beginning with *Swami and Friends*. Swaminathan, the man protagonist in the novel is a mere school-going child who is portrayed by Narayan as a bold and confident boy who will not accept any teaching without logic. In fact, his impressionable mind is hurt when the teacher is abusive of the 'Hindu Gods' and makes fun of them in class. The *Rajas Guna* of desire for learning, questioning and rational thinking is portrayed beautifully in Swami's rather apt response when Narayan writes:

> He paused for breath. The teacher was intolerable today. Swaminathan's blood boiled. He got up and asked, "if he did not, why was he crucified?" The teacher told him that he might come to him at the end of the period and learn it in private. Emboldened by this mild reply, Swaminathan put to him another question, "If he was a god, why did he eat flesh and fish and drink wine?" As a *brahmin* boy it was inconceivable to him that a god should be a non-vegetarian. In answer to this, Ebenezar left his seat, advanced slowly towards Swaminathan and tried to wrench his left ear off (4-5).

Swaminathan is passionate about his relationship with his friends. He is the child- hero of the novel studying in the Albert Mission School in Malgudi, situated on the bank of river, Sarayu. The river has a bridge over it and from the windows of school one can see trains passing over it. Autobiographical strains in Narayan's writings are seen when he portrays Swami as an average student. However, his school life is not entirely unhappy for he has four good friends. A detailed pen-portraits of these friends are traced by Narayan. One of them is Somu, the monitor of the class. He is confident and calm, friendly with the teachers. 'No teacher ever put to him a question in the class. It could not be said he shone brilliantly as student. It was believed that only the headmaster could reprimand him. He was more or less the uncle of the class' (6-7). Mani is 'the Mighty Good For Nothing' (7) boy who is feared and admired by all. He is a sort of bully and says that his strength lies in the 'pair of wooden clubs he has at home and with which he can easily break the neck of those that dared to tamper with him' (7).

The third friend is Sankar, the most brilliant boy of the class. He gets marks as high as ninety percent and can answer any question that is put to him. However, there are those who feel that he gets such high marks by flattering the teachers and by doing menial work for them. Swami has no doubts about his ability and considers him to be a marvel: 'He could speak to the teachers in English in the open class. He knew the names of all the rivers, mountains and countries in the world. He could repeat history in his sleep. Grammar was child's play to him. His face was radiant with intelligence' (8).

Swami's fourth friend is Samuel, called the pea, because of his small size. There is nothing uncommon about him, for he is neither a good student, nor physically remarkable. The only 'bond between them was laughter. They were able to see together the same absurdities and incongruities in things. The most trivial and unnoticeable things to others would tickle them to death' (8).

Rajam, the new boy's entry in the novel sees Swami being impressed by his carefree conduct, manners, clothing and by his brilliance as a student: 'He dressed very well. He was the only boy in the class who wore socks and shoes, fur cap and tie and wonderful coat and knickers' (14). Swaminathan is desirous of Rajam's friendship as he is impressed by Rajam's ways: 'If Mani jabbed, Rajam jabbed; if Mani clouted, he clouted; if Mani kicked, he kicked. If Mani was the overlored of the class, Rajam seemed to be nothing less. And add to all this the fact that Rajam was a regular seventy-percenter, second only to Shankar. These were sure indications that Rajam was the new power in the class' (15).

The *Rajas Guna* of desire is portrayed wonderfully by Narayan when he shows how impressionable the young minds are and how they get swayed easily with the underlying desire for power, intelligence and position. This is a measure which is often used by adults to decide on their friendship with others.

In the novel, *The Bachelor of Arts*, the man protagonist, Chandran is totally under the *Rajas Guna* of desire and passion. At the start of the novel, he is an Indian college student, who completes his graduation, falls in love and receives a disappointment. During the course of the story, he goes on to become a sanyasi and learns to live a life free of illusions. However, since he is still under the impact of the *Rajas Guna* of passion and lust, his brief phase as a sanyasi fails. Finally, he returns from sanyas, takes up a job and gets married to a beautiful girl chosen by his parents. In addition to the chain of events that make up the mosaic called life in this novel, it is also the journey of Chandran's attempt to come on his own and to carve a niche for himself in the intriguing world of adults.

The novel opens and the man protagonist, Chandran is introduced as a young man under the influence of *Rajas Guna* of desire for pleasure of the flesh. He is shown going to a movie with his friend. Narayan writes:

> Chandran stopped at a 'shop to buy some betel leaves and a packet of cigarettes. Attending a night show was not an ordinary affair. Chandran was none of your business-like automatons who go to a cinema, sit there and return home. It was an aesthetic experience to be approached with due preparation. You had to chew the betel leaves and nut, chew gently, until the heart was stimulated and threw out delicate beads of perspiration and caused a fine tingling sensation behind the ears; on top of that you had to light a cigarette, inhale the fumes and with the night breeze blowing on your perspiring forehead, go to the cinema, smoke more cigarettes there, see the picture and from there go to an hotel nearby for hot coffee at midnight, take some more betel leaves and cigarette and go home and sleep. This was the ideal way to set about night show. Chandran squeezed the maximum aesthetic delight out of the experience and Ramu's company was most important to him. It was his presence that gave sense of completion to things. He too smoked, chewed, drank coffee, laughed (he was the greatest laughter in the world), admired Chandran, ragged him quarrelled

> with him, breathed delicious scandal over the names of his professors and friends and unknown people (13).

Further, when they spot Brown with a girl, Chandran comments that perhaps she is his wife. When Ramu replies in the negative, he says, "Must be some other girl, then. The white fellows are born to enjoy life. Our people really don't know how to live. If a person is seen with a girl by his side, a hundred eyes stare at him and a hundred tongues comment, whereas no European ever goes out without taking a girl with him" (15). Chandran's desire of want of comfort gets highlighted when he says, "When I start earning, I shall buy a car first of all. Nothing like it. You can just see the picture and go straight to bed" (17).

The story unfolds and Chandran's passion for the fifteen-year-old Malathi leaves him full of her thoughts so much so that he does 'not have room for anything else in his mind' (54). Narayan, the master story teller, showcases the *Rajas Guna* of passion and lust when he writes:

> That night he (Chandran) went home very preoccupied. It was at five o'clock that he had met her and at nine he was still thinking of her. After dinner he did not squat on the carpet in the hall, but preferred to go to his room and remain alone there. He tried to read a little; he was in the middle of Well's Tono Bungay. He had found the book gripping, but now he felt it was obtrusive. He was irritated. He put away the book and sat staring at the wall. He presently realised that darkness would be more soothing. He blew out the lamp and sat in his chair (56-7).

Chandran's passion for Malathi grows and he starts to take care of his personal appearance in great detail. He shaves with care and pays attention to his hair while awaiting the evening. He dresses in his best clothes and spends two hours on the banks of the river waiting for her arrival. She does not come and when he sets for home, he feels his 'shave, ironed tweed coat, were all wasted' (57). When Chandran sees her at river bank the next evening, he notices that she is attired in green sari and is 'drawn towards her as if drawn by a rope' (59). The desire for her makes him want to stare at her. 'Staring was half the victory in love....and if you don't start an eye friendship immediately, you may not get the opportunity again for a million years' (60). His desire to contact her makes him find out her house. Through Mohan's co-operation Chandran learns that his 'sweetheart's name was Malathi, that she was unmarried and that she was the daughter of Mr. D.W. Krishna Iyer, Head Clerk in the Executive Engineer's office' (67).

The *Rajas Guna of Passion*, lust and desire for Malathi knows no bounds in Chandran's mind who, even though is not yet independent and settled in life, finds courage and talks to his father about his own marriage proposal to Malathi. His emotions are at their peak and thinking of her in the darkness, he is seen moaning: "Darling, what are you doing? Do you hear me?" (79). He does not want his mother to pose difficulty in marriage by her unreasonable demands of dowry and argues with her: "You care more for your status than for the happiness of your son" (84).

Chandran is devastated when Malathi's parents find a fault in his horoscope and reject the marriage. Fighting his parents' wishes, Malathi's parents' rejection and going against the logical thinking which is becoming of a man, he gives in to his desire of possessing Malathi as his wife and tries luck one last time, hoping to get it right in his 'last chance' (90). However, luck fails him. His letter remains undelivered and Malathi gets married to someone else.

Narayan's spell of *Rajas Guna* of one-sided love and desire unfolds yet another journey of Chandran's life in the chapters that follow in the novel.

Dr B.P. Singh writes:

> Practically the whole part two of *The Bachelor of Arts* is devoted to the problem of love and marriage. There is nothing of sex in it. It is only the passion of love that is dominant throughout (R.K. Narayan and Social Vision: 57).

In Narayan's next novel, the man protagonist, Mr. Sampath comes under the influence of *Rajas Guna* due to his desire for money and passion for the woman protagonist, Shanti. In the beginning, Mr. Sampath is shown to be a sensible man taking the responsibility of his family and questioning his identity, pondering over, 'till I know who I am, how can I know what I should do?' (13). He is seen arguing

'I don't see much difference between a ghost and a living person. All of us are skin-covered ghosts, for that matter (17). However, the predominating *Rajas Guna* of desire for money takes over his entire persona. His work as a printer revolves not as much around printing as around fabricating tales and making money. In his words:

> It's my duty to see that *The Banner* is out again. Please wait. I will see that the journal is set up on a lino machine and printed off a rotary and dispatched in truck-loads every week. For this we need a lot of money. Don't you doubt it for a moment. I am going to make a lot of money… (88-9).

When, due to reasons of delay, the printing of the weekly, *The Banner*, is suspended, Mr. Sampath embarks on a new venture of making a motion picture. The entire focus of the film is pleasures of the flesh and is named *The Burning of Kama*. Mr. Sampath's lust of money is so much that he shoots the heroine using beams of light in such a manner that the curves of her body are revealed.

> ….Srinivas noted how cunningly they had managed to make her clothes unnecessary by the No. 10 light, which shot up a beam of illumination from behind her at ground level. "What ingenuity" he commented to himself. Her body stood out as if X-rayed, her necklace and diadem glittered and shone and seemed to be the only apparel she wore. Every one, the principals in canvas chairs, went over to the camera to look through the view-finder and shake their heads with academic approval (186).

He gets involved with the heroine, Shanti so much that Srinivas suspects that 'Sampath hardly went home nowadays, spending all his time in the studio and running about, completely lost in his new interests (144). Ravi confirms the *Rajas Guna* of passion and lust in Mr. Sampath when he observes, "I see her (Shanti) going home every day, sitting close to Sampath and touching him; they are always together" (175). So lost is Mr. Sampath in his rendezvous with Shanti that he ignores his wife who is seen 'crying for days' (177). When Srinivas confronts Sampath, his reply is:

> Some people say that every sane man needs two wives— a perfect one for the house and a perfect one outside for social life….I have the one. Why not the other? I have confidence that I will keep

> both of them happy and if necessary in separate houses. Is a man's heart so narrow that it cannot accommodate more than one? I have married according to Vedic rites: let me have one according to the civil marriage law... (179).

Further, when he is chided for *Rajas Guna* of passion and lust for Shanti, the argument he has with Srinivas is portrayed by Narayan thus:

> "Oh, these women will make a scene. She will be all right. She must get used to it."
>
> .... "Let me be frank: I'm convinced that you are merely succumbing to a little piece of georgette, powder and curves. You have no right to cause any unhappiness to your wife and children.
>
> "Well, sir," Sampath said with mock humility. Here goes my solemn declaration that my wife and children shall lack nothing in life either in affection or comfort. Will this satisfy you? If I buy Shanti a car, my wife shall have another; if I give her a house, I will give the other also a house; it will really be a little expensive duplicating everything this way, but I won't mind it. Later on, when they see how much it is costing me, I'm sure they will bury the hatchet and become friends again… (180).

The Guide is yet another masterpiece of R.K. Narayan's novels. The character of man protagonist, Raju, has been carved out in way which shows the predominance of *Rajas Guna*. His journey from childhood to adult life, makes him undergo experiences where he lives without adhering to social ethics. Raju is an outgoing, resourceful, romantic and materialistic young man whose heart rules his head. In a long series of unscrupulous acts, he deceives Marco, gets romantically involved with his wife, Rosie, drives his old widowed mother out of the house, forges Rosie's signature for wealth and worse, plays with the beliefs of innocent villagers. Rosie is introduced to us first in the words (and eyes) of Raju when he says:

"Don't imagine on hearing her name that she wore a short skirt or cropped her hair. She looked just the orthodox dancer that she was. She wore saris of bright hues and gold lace, had curly hair which she braided and beflowered, wore diamond ear-rings and a heavy gold necklace. I told her at the first opportunity what a great dancer she was and how she fostered our cultural traditions, and it pleased her (9).

The predominance of *Rajas Guna* of desire and passion overpowers Raju's character when on seeing her, he finds her 'so lovely and elegant' (65). Even though Raju is aware that she is a married lady, he discards his 'khaki bush-coat and dhoti' and takes the trouble to make himself presentable by wearing a 'silk jibba and lace dhoti' and grooming himself so well that even his mother remarks: 'ah, like a bridegroom!' (65). Raju is aware of Rosie's body. He notices how 'she stretched out her arm slightly and swayed it in imitation of the movement; she swayed her whole body to the rhythm.... (68) Later he is remanded of her 'scent filled presence' (69). When he returns home, Raju misses out on no opportunity to flirt with her. He says, "Don't you know my voice?". When she asks who is on the door. He is observant of her: 'she looked dishevelled, her eyes were red with recent tears and she wore a faded cotton sari: no paint or perfume, but I was prepared to accept her as she was' (72).

Raju is overwhelmed by his lust for her and he admits 'life is so blank without your presence' (73). In his words:

> ...she suddenly darted forward and forcibly snatched it away from my hand. Oh! That touch made my head reel for a moment. I didn't see clearly. Everything disappeared into a sweet, dark haze, as under chloroform. My memory dwelt on the touch all through the dinner. I was not aware what we were eating or what they were saying. I sat with bowed head. I was nervous to see her face and meet her looks. I don't recollect when we finished eating and when she took away the dishes. I was only conscious of her soft movements, my thoughts dwelt on her golden touch.... (77).
>
> Further:
>
> .... Oh, the whispers, the stars and the darkness – I began to breathe heavily with excitement.
>
> 'Have you caught a cold'? She asked.
>
> I said, 'No'.
>
> 'Why are you breathing so noisily'?

> I wanted to put my face close to her and whisper, 'your dance was marvellous. You are gifted. Do it again sometime. God bless you. Won't you be my sweetheart?' (79).
>
> Raju's head rules his head and is in a frenzied state by his passion for Rosie that he is prepared to ruin himself.

He pines for her 'every hour' (84). He lures her into a relationship with him by playing on her emotions. He knows her weakness for dancing and uses it for his personal interests. He tells her, "I am really very unhappy to think of you, such a gem lost to the world" (86). He draws Rosie to himself by taking her all over the place, 'showing her the town hall tower'; showing her Sarayu and sitting on the sands and munching 'a large packet of salted nuts' (87). He returns with her to the hotel room when it is 'nearing mid night' (88) and seduces the already delirious Rosie by gently pushing 'her out of the way' and stepping in and locking 'the door on the world' (89). Raju confesses to be 'obsessed with thoughts of Rosie' (115). For a brief period when Raju thinks he will not be able to meet Rosie again, he says:

> I cannot remember more miserable period of my life. The usual symptoms were present, of course: no taste for food, no sound sleep, no stability (I couldn't stay put in any one place) no peace of mind, no sweetness of temper or speech- no, no, no, a number of nos. With all seriousness, I returned to my normal avocation. But everything looked so unreal (136).

As the story proceeds, Marco gets to know of his wife's affair with Raju and leaves her alone while he goes away to Madras. Rosie then comes to live with Raju. So strong is Raju's *Rajas Guna* of passion, desire and lust for Rosie that he allows the married Rosie to believe what she is doing is correct. Despite his own mother's opposition, he reassures her:

> .... you are in the right place. Forget all your past. We will teach that cad a lesson by and by. I made a grandiose announcement, first, I'll make the world recognise you as the greatest artist of the time (153).

He admits that 'living with Rosie under the same roof was enough' for him and that he 'wanted nothing more in life' (161). This, not only because he is desirous of her body, but also because he sees in her 'a gold-mine' (162).

Rosie is a good dancer and Raju encourages her to practice dance regularly. When she invites him to see her dance and evaluate it critically, he obliges, albeit because of his lust for her:

> I watched her critically, but what I watched were the curves that tempted me to hug her on the spot. However, my mother was passing in and out and nowadays we had to seize our romantic moments and get through with it at odd times – for instance, when my mother went to fetch water. We knew exactly how long she would be away and utilised it. It was all irksome, but very novel and made me forget my troubles. Whenever I watched her sway her figure, if there was no one about I constantly interrupted her performance, although I was supposed to watch her from an art critic's point of view (163).

Raju arranges for her first performance on stage on the occasion of Albert Mission *Boys' Annual Social*. He launches Rosie with a new name Nalini. By and by Rosie becomes extremely popular because she is tremendously talented. However, the *Rajas Guna* of desire is so predominant in the man protagonist Raju that he believes to have 'made' Rosie. The journey of Raju in the novel portrays other influences of the *Rajas Guna* on him viz. action, ambition to earn money, vices such as drinking and gambling, cheating, forgery etc. Till the end he is caught up in the web of *Rajas Guna* when due to a turn of events he finds his motive and meaning of life.

Thus, the men protagonists in the above novels are influenced by the *Rajas Guna* of **Desire, Passion and Lust.**

Attachment

Attachment is another quality which comes under the rubric of *Rajas Guna*. Attachment is described as being fond of a certain thing or another person. It also means having affection or liking for the other. Attachment can also be understood in comparison with its opposite 'detachment'. The Hindu view of detachment means the ultimate state of being 'in the moment'. In other words, while one is responsible and active, one does not worry over the past or future. The detachment is towards the result of one's actions rather than towards everything in life. This concept is cited extensively within Puranic and Vedic literature, for example:

> One who performs his duty without attachment, surrendering the results unto the Supreme Lord, is unaffected by sinful action, as the lotus is untouched by water (*Bhagvad Gita*).

One of the biggest contributions of Hinduism and Buddhism is the teaching that all human suffering is due to the bonds of attachment one experiences, to others and to material things. When the object of attachment is separated, the experience is suffering, pain and grief. It is to address and overcome this chronic, inevitable human suffering of loss, that the teachings ask humans to put aside attachment and to become 'detached' from the object of desire.

In Narayan's novel *Swami and Friends,* the protagonist Swaminathan shows the *Rajas Guna* of attachment to his parents and peer group. Narayan weaves a simple and charming story set in the 1930s of ten-year old Swaminathan and his experiences of growing up in Malgudi. Autobiographical traits of Narayan in the story are evident as Swami, is made to dislike the constraints of conventional school and education. Instead, he loves to spend time with his friends. Swami is also very attached to his grandmother. Besides he has a remarkable bonding with his four friends- Somu, Mani, Sankar and Samuel. All four share a common trait- their ability to laugh at everything! *Rajas Guna* of attachment to Rajam, the new boy at school impacts Swami's mind. He notices little details about Rajam:

> He (Rajam) was a newcomer; he dressed very well, he was the only boy in class who wore socks and shoes, fur cap and tie and wonderful coat and knickers. He came to the school in a car.... He spoke very good English, exactly like a European; which meant that few in the school could make out what he said (14).

Despite the differences, Swami seems to like Rajam. He is loving and loyal towards Rajam. *Rajas Guna* of attachment is highlighted when Swami starts coming for cricket practice to please Rajam even if it means missing his drill class. Swami gets into trouble for playing truant. Further, Swami runs away from home in a moment of desperation and gets lost on the way, thereby missing the cricket match for which he had been practicing for many days. Rajam gets annoyed and refuses to see Swami. Shortly afterwards Rajam's father is transferred. Swami is shattered by this knowledge as he is extremely attached to Rajam.

Rajam and his parents are to leave Malgudi by the train on Tuesday morning. Mani gives Swami the sad news only on Monday night as Rajam strictly forbids Mani to tell anything to Swami. Swami is pained and hurt, but reaches the station on time. He carries with him Anderson's Fairy Tales to give it to Rajam as a 'parting present'. However, he is not able to not talk to Rajam, for he and his parents are surrounded throughout by the police and district officers of Malgudi. The parting of Rajam with his erstwhile friends is the most poignant scene in the book:

> At the sight of the familiar face Swaminanthan lost control of himself and cried: 'Oh Rajam, Rajam you are going away. When will you come back?' Rajam kept looking at him without a word and then (as it seems to Swaminathan) opened his mouth to say something, when everything was disturbed by the guard's blast and the hoarse whistle of the engine……Rajam's face with the words still unuttered on his lips, receded (211).

The *Rajas Guna* of attachment influences the protagonist Swaminathan and is the cause of his thoughts and actions.

The novel, *The English Teacher* unfolds the story of the man protagonist Krishna who comes under the influence of *Rajas Guna* on many accounts. He is attached to his wife and daughter. He is also attached to his work as a teacher. However, when his wife Sushila dies, the desire to reunite with her makes him undergo a series of events which have no rationale or logical thinking.

S.K. Biswal's observation of Krishna, the man protagonist in *The English Teacher* is thus:

> Krishna, the central character in *The English Teacher*, by R.K. Narayan undertakes an emotional, intellectual and spiritual journey during the course of the novel. At the start of the novel he is an English teacher, living and teaching at the same school where he was once a pupil and at the end we see him learning to communicate

psychically with his dead wife. He learns and changes during the course of the novel in a way which we could not have predicted at the beginning. Krishna's change comes about not as a result of any grand plan or ambition, but as a result of his response to a series of challenging circumstances which arise once he begins to take steps away from the cloistered and protective environment of his school (56-7).

Narayan's recording in his Memoir *My Days* of the event of his wife's death deserves attention here. He writes:

> More than any other book, *The English Teacher,* is autobiographical in content, very little part of it being fiction. The English Teacher of the novel, Krishna is a fictional character in the fictional city of Malgudi; but he goes through the same experience I had gone through and he calls his wife Susila and the child is Leela instead of Hema. The toll that typhoid took and all the desolation that followed, with a child to look after and the psychic adjustments, are based on my own experience...The dedication of the book to the memory of my wife should to some extent give the reader a clue that the book may not be all fiction (150-151).

The novel is divided into two parts, the first half being an interesting account of Krishna's domestic life. Krishna is shown as a Lecturer in English at Albert Mission College. The *Rajas Guna* of attachment is predominant in him. Initially when his wife Susila is not living with him, Krishna awaits her letters. On receiving one, he smells the letter 'before opening it.... (for) it carries with it the 'fragrance of her trunk' (20). Krishna fondly remembers that 'a mild jasmine smell surrounded her and all possessions ever since (he) had known her.' (20). Later when Susila plans to come and stay with him, he is excited. Keeping her comfort in mind, he wants a house. He says:

> I must have a house… which faces south, for its breeze, keeps out the western sun, gets in the eastern and admits the due measure of northen light that artists so highly value. The house must have a room for each one of us and for a guest or two. It must keep us all together and yet separate us when we would rather not see each other's faces….we must have helpful people and good people near at hand, but obnoxious neighbours ten miles away. It must be within

> walking distance of college and yet so far out as to let me enjoy my domestic life free from professional intrusions (23).

So influential is the *Rajas Guna* of attachment to his wife that Krishna shudders at the fate that might await Susila in the few weeks his own mother plans to come and stay with them trying to help them run the house. He rationalises:

> My wife was the last daughter of the family and was greatly petted by her parents, in her own house, where she spent most of her time reading, knitting, embroiding or looking after a garden. In spite of it, after my marriage my mother kept her in the village and trained her up in house keeping (29).

He admires Susila for being his 'cash keeper' and managing the accounts in such an efficient manner that 'a hundred rupees seemed to do the work of two hundred' (39). Further, when he finds himself at a loss for subjects to write on, the idea of making his beautiful wife a subject interests him. The *Rajas Guna* of attachment is so strong in Krishna that he promises to take her to, not only, on an all-India tour sometimes, but also to England and Europe whenever he made 'a lot of money of the books (he was) going to write' (55). Krishna imagines how Susila 'would touch the marble of Taj, stand astounded before the snow-covered Himalayas and before the crowd and magnitude of European cities (56).

Krishna wants to give her domestic bliss and for Susila's comfort, he decides to buy a house. In sync with his motive, he takes her along to see a house. However, as circumstances would have it, Susila has to use a lavatory which is infested with flies and unfortunately, she gets down with typhoid. Though Krishna tries his best to save her, Susila dies. When Krishna takes her for cremation, the *Rajas Guna* of extreme attachment to his wife leaves him devastated. Narayan writes:

> ...they build up a pyre, place her on it, cover her up with layers of fuel...Leaving only face and the part of her chest out, four layers deep down. I pour ghee on and drop the fire......There are no more surprises and shocks in life, so that I watch the flame without agitation. For me the greatest reality is this and nothing else.... nothing else will worry or interest me in life hereafter (96).

Krishna's mind is ever occupied with thoughts and memories of his dead wife so much so that in the darkness he often feels an echo of her voice and sometimes hears her delirious talk in sick bed.

The novel takes a turn and in time Krishna receives a message from a man saying he can connect with spirits. In fact, the second half of the novel is devoted to the psychic communion of the man protagonist with the spirit of his dead wife. In his interview with Ved Mehta, Narayan said that "all that he has set down in the second half of *The English Teacher* had actually happened to him and that he would frequently visit a lawyer in Madras who claimed to communicate with the dead through so called automatic writing." Krishna contacts the man and is willingly sucked into the act of calling and communicating with the spirit of his dead wife. Krishna seems happy with this, although when the so called Godman produces sheet after sheet covered with pencil's scribbling, not a word of it can be deciphered. Despite the illegible handwriting, Krishna is happy to be able to communicate with his wife. He says:

> Nowadays I went about my work with a light heart. I felt as if a dead load had been lifted. The day seemed full of possibilities of surprise and joy. At home I devoted myself to my studies more energetically. The sense of futility was leaving me. I attended to my work earnestly (120).

On the contrary, when due to some reasons, Krishna is not able to meet his friend and thus not able to communicate with his wife, he finds life so worthless that he contemplates committing suicide. He says:

> A long dip in this river, or a finger poked into a snake hole - there are two thousand ways of ending this misery. But the child, the child…She will be looked after by God and by everyone. She is an entity. She was able to go on without her mother and she could equally well carry on without her father. I have put by a little money for her…far off I saw the glow of a funeral pyre over the walls of the cremation ground and I sighed for it. It seemed to be the greatest aspiration one could have. "Exactly where she was placed and burnt…". I recollected her pale face, with the flies on it and the smile on her lips and broke down at the memory.

> I recovered and said to myself: "this is also my end. Oh, God, send me to those flames at once." I saw a picture of myself being carried there and the funeral ceremonies and this vision seemed to give me a little peace.
>
> Thus, days followed, bleak, dreary and unhappy days, with a load on the mind. I felt as though I had been filled with molten lead (151).

The *Rajas Guna* of attachment impacts the man protagonist in his relationship with his daughter, Leela too. After Susila's demise, Krishna refuses to 'allow her to be taken away by her grand parents'(97). He bathes her with expert hands, braids her hair and washes and look after her clothes and keeps correct count of her jackets and skirts. He slips into the double role of a father and mother with great expertise. His one aim in life is to see that 'she does not feel the absence of her mother' (97). When his mother reprimands Krishna saying he was unpractical and stubborn, he replies, "God intends me to learn these things and do them efficiently, I can't shirk it... (98).

He spends as much time as is possible with his daughter. He feels guilty when due to his college work and the extra activities, he is unable to give time to Leela. He prays to God to save him 'from becoming too absorbed in anything to look after the child properly' (133). Leela joins school and the headmaster shows Krishna a green boat made by Leela on the very first day she came to school. He tells Krishna that 'she finished it within an hour'. Krishna is filled with pride and satisfaction. He almost gets teary- eyed and feels: 'my little Leela in relation to an outside world, making her own mark on it' (134).

The *Rajas Guna* of attachment is so strong in him that he is opposed to the idea of sending his daughter away even with her grandmother. However, for Leela's sake, he agrees. When she is travelling by bus, Krishna's anxiety is portrayed by Narayan as he writes:

> I felt acute anxiety about sending her by bus. I had never been separated from her; the thought appalled me. But as I saw her bubbling over with enthusiasm I told myself: "Don't be selfish. She must have her own life."...I had been dinning into my mother's ears instructions regarding the child. Even as the conductor blew his whistle I shouted instructions. "Don't allow her to lean out.

See that she doesn't eat too many sweets. She gets a racking cough at nights. Oil and bath every Friday, but the water must not be too hot...She must be immediately wrapped up...Milk, only half a tumbler..." My mother merely smiled (175-6).

To please his innermost self, Krishna resigns from his job as a college teacher. He plans to 'write poetry and live and work with children and watch their minds unfold...." (180). Narayan winds up this sensitive novel with Krishna's quest for inner peace. However, till the last page of the book, the *Rajas Guna* of attachment to his wife Susila remains strong. He pines for her. He imagines her to be with him always. He still buys jasmine flowers for her, knowing well that she is no more.

Narayan writes in a manner which is heart-wrenching:

......I softly called "Susila! Susila, my wife..." with all my being. It sounded as if it were a hypnotic melody. "My wife...my wife, my wife..." My mind trembled with this rhythm; I forgot myself and my own existence. I fell into a drowse, whispering, "My wife, wife." How long? How could I say? When I opened my eyes again she was sitting on my bed looking at me with an extraordinary smile in her eyes.

"Susila! Susila!" I cried. "You here!" "Yes, I'm here, have always been here." I sat up leaning on my pillow. "Why do you disturb yourself?" she asked.

"I am making a place for you," I said, edging away a little. I looked her up and down and said: "How well you look!" her complexion had a golden glow, her eyes sparkled with a new light, her saree shimmered with blue interwoven with "light" as she had termed it..."How beautiful!" I said looking at it. "Yes, I always wear this when I come to you. I know you like it very much," she said. I gazed on her face. There was an overwhelming fragrance of jasmine surrounding her. "Still jasmine scented!" I commented.

...It was a moment of rare, immutable joy—a moment for which one feels grateful to Life and Death (183-4).

Nityananda Pattanayak highlights the *Rajas Guna* of attachment in Krishna when he writes:

> By the time Narayan began to write *The English Teacher* he had undergone a great psychic development following the untimely death of his wife and his subsequent reconciliation to it. This had its effect on his views on schemes of life that, in turn, made a strong impact on his conception of human time. Once his views on human life on the material plane got changed, his conception of time also underwent a transformation and he portrayed time more and more from Indian classical angle which is mythical and regenerative. He began to believe that "Everything is bound to come out right in the end; if not in this world, at least in other worlds." This counterpoise of human time with mythical time is not found here for the first time; it is also visible, albeit faintly, in his first novel where Swami prays for the salvation of the soul of an ant. But what is significant here, in comparison to his earlier novels, is the assured application of the mythical time (78).

Thus, the personality trait of men protagonists in the respective novels is cemented in the *Rajas Guna* of **Attachment** and is the cause of their responses and actions.

Obedience

Obedience as described by the Oxford Dictionary means willingness to do what one is told to do. It is synonymous with being amenable, dutiful and compliant. On one hand it leads to making of law abiding and dutiful citizens who are well behaved and compliant, on the other it may also develop personalities who are submissive, subservient and tamed. Thus, obedience to the commands of preceptors and parents may reflect one's desire to conform to other person's wishes with an intention to please despite the command being right or wrong. Preceptors simply means a general rule about how to behave and what to think. Many a times, thus, the awareness of right and wrong is compromised. This characteristic is a chief quality of the *Rajas Guna* for it is closely related to desire and attachment.

In the novel *Swami and Friends*, the man protagonist Swaminathan shows the *Rajas Guna* of obedience. The authenticity and credibility of Narayan's treatment of school life arises from the fact that it is rooted in his own personal experiences. Narayan never went to England, never studied in English schools and colleges. His early childhood experiences left vivid impression on his mind. This makes his account of school life real and convincing. Most of the Indian boys do not live in hostels, but are day scholars and pass as much time at home as in school. Hence in *Swami and friends*, sufficient space has been devoted to Swami's home life and relationship with his parents and grandmother. He is not a bright student, not eager to acquire knowledge. Every Monday for him is a 'black Monday'. The teachers are shown to be strict with room only for conformity. Unable to bear this tyranny, he runs away from the Albert Mission School and then from Board High School. One of the major themes in R.K. Narayan's novels is family relationships. As Williams Walsh point out;

> The family is the immediate context in which his sensibility operates and his novels are remarkable for the subtlety and conviction with which family relationships are treated that of son and parents and brother and brother in *The Bachelor of Arts*, of husband and wife and father and daughter in *The English Teacher*, of father and son in *The Financial Expert* and of grandmother and grandson in *Waiting for the Mahatma*. The closeness of relationship between the adults and children and the absence of watertight compartments between the worlds of the two, constitute the basis of these novels. However, the action is developed on the conflict between the egocentricity of an individual member and family's claim on him.

Humour is coupled with the *Rajas Guna* of obedience when Narayan portrays the character of the tender Swaminathan in such a way that he is made to believe that all elders, when they say something, have a deeper meaning and Swami must adhere to it. When for instance, his question paper mentions the question, 'What moral do you infer from the story of the Brahmin and the tiger?', he feels that it must have one since the question paper mentions it. In his innocence (and the cheeky humour of Narayan) he comes up with two morals 'We must never accept a gold bangle when it is offered by a tiger or love of gold bangle costs one one's life (69). Later when the exams are approaching, his father reprimands him, "Suppose you fail? … and, "Suppose you fail and all your class-mates go up, leaving you behind?...

Suppose all your juniors in the Fifth standard become your class-mates?" (58) Swaminathan, with his *Rajas Guna* of obedience, sits at decimals for half an hour.

The *Rajas Guna* of obedience impacts the man protagonist. As a school boy, Swami finds staying at home in the evenings extremely irksome. He longs for the sandbanks of Sarayu and Mani's (his friend) company, but since his father forbids him to go out till the examinations are over, Swami does not venture out. To please his father, Swami obeys him and sits with his books for long hours. In fact, when he hears his father say, "That is right, boy," Swaminathan feels 'that the moment was worth all his suffering' (64).

With obedience, comes fear of authority and failure to reason accurately. When Swaminathan gives a list of things to be bought for his forthcoming exam and tells his father that his examinations begin the day after, the father shouts, "And yet you are wandering about the house like an unleashed donkey! What preposterous list is this? Do you think rupees, annas and paise drop from the sky?" (67). *Rajas Guna* of obedience highlights the personality of protagonist in all his relationships with his elders. In school, when Swaminathan fails to go to school, the entire episode portrayed by Narayan shows the Indian system of upbringing of children wherein conformity and obedience is regarded very valuable. Narayan writes:

> ……the headmaster shouted, "won't you open your mouth?" he brought the cane sharply down on Swaminathan's right shoulder. Swaminathan kept staring at the master with tearful eyes, massaging with his left hand the spot where the cane was laid. "I will kill you if you keep on staring without answering my question," cried the headmaster (124).

In the Indian context, the *Rajas Guna* of obedience is considered to be a value and Narayan portrays the men protagonists in most of his novels under the impact of this *Guna.* In the novel, *The Bachelor of Arts*, the protagonist Chandran shows the impact of *Rajas Guna* of obedience throughout the novel. Due to his Indian upbringing where the children are taught to respect and conform to their elders' wishes without questioning them, Narayan writes in a manner which brings out this trait in his man protagonist.

So afraid is the twenty-one-year-old Chandran of his father that on returning home late, he does not want to come face to face with his father. Narayan writes:

> Chandran came to his gate, he saw his father in the veranda, pacing up and down. Late-coming was one of the few things that upset him. Chandran hesitated for a moment before lifting the gate chain. He opened the gate a little, slipped in and put the chain back on it's hook noiselessly. His usual move after this would be to slip round to the back door and enter the house without his father's knowledge. But now he had a surge of self-respect. He realised that what he usually did was a piece of evasive cowardice worthy of an adolescent, he was not eighteen but twenty-one (11).

Chandran as an adult is not made to make his own decisions. Even if he wishes to go for a night show movie with his friends, he is apprehensive of his father's reaction because 'Father never encouraged any one to attend a night show' for he considerd them to be 'very bad for the health' (12). Like a young school boy, the adult man protagonist, Chandran obeys his father. When exams are approaching, he sets an alarm at four-thirty in the morning not only to study, but more so to please his father. Chandran is seen explaining to his father:

> You see, Father, but for this dreadful meeting. I should have done ninety hours of study, according to my time-table. I shall still make it up. I shall not be available to any one from tomorrow (40).

Chandran is so much under the influence of the *Rajas Guna* of obedience that he listens to his father even though he mumbles otherwise:

> Father said to Chandran: "Take the gate key and open the gate. How can he get out?"
>
> "If you leave him alone, he will jump over the wall and go," mumbled Chandran sourly as he took the gate key from the nail on the veranda wall (44).

The South-Indian upbringing of Narayan makes him portray the man protagonist as hesitating to broach the subject of his own marriage to his father. Chandran prays to God to give him courage and goes to his father to talk to him about his marriage, but his courage fails him at the last moment. He regrets his cowardice, unworthy of Malathi (his sweetheart) and calls himself a 'spineless worm' (68). In his own words:

> Afraid of a father! He was not a baby asking for a toy, but a full-grown adult out on serious business, very serious business (68).

The rational side of Chandran questions: "why should we be cudgelled and nose-led by our elders?......Why can't we be allowed to arrange our lives as we please? Why can't they leave us to rise or sink on our own ideals?" (71) However, the *Rajas Guna* of obedience impacts his personality and makes him a conformist. When he is offered alcohol by his friends, he refuses. Even after persuasion, Chandran remains firm. In his opinion, he was being asked to 'commit the darkest crime' since he has made 'a vow never to touch alcohol in my life before my mother' (98).

Chandran is shown obeying his father even when he wants to take up a job and his father disagrees on his choice of the job of becoming a government servant. The father wants to send him to England, but later agrees to his wife's advice of sending Chandran to Madras to her relatives. When Chandran is preparing to travel to Madras for the second time, the father still treats Chandran as a child, brings for him a half of dozen handkerchiefs, a pair of new *dhoties*, a woollen scarf and requests Chandran to hand it over to his brother. Chandran takes up a job the newspaper *The Daily Messenger,* returns to Malgudi and sets up his own office. The *Rajas Guna* of obedience is predominant in Chandran's personality. Later in the novel, he agrees to marry the girl of his parent's choice, Mr Jayarama Iyer's daughter, Susila.

The *Rajas Guna* of **Obedience**, hence makes the men protagonists dutiful, compliant and submissive.

Ambition and Action

Ambition and Action involve the process of doing something, typically to achieve an aim. It is synonymous with activity, movement, work, effort, exertion and operation, all of which involve frenzied activity, a typical trait of the *Rajas Guna.* Men protagonists under the impact of ambition and action are forced to react, exploit others or manoeuvre situations keeping in mind their own interests. To achieve and accomplish goals, they are a part of effort and activity. Ambition is often closely associated with the love of fame and power. Power is the ability to influence or control the behaviour of people. Power can be seen as evil or unjust, but the exercise of power is accepted as endemic to humans as social beings.

In the novel, *The Bachelor of Arts,* Narayan's protagonist Chandran shows the predominating mode of *Rajas Guna* of ambition and action. The novel is broadly divided into four sections. All the parts have significant portrayal of the *Rajas Guna* of action. When Chandran is a student, aspiring to become a Bachelor of Arts, he is shown to be under the impact of action for the pleasure of flesh viz. movies and cigarettes. When he gets attracted to Malathi, he is shown pining for her with passion and lust. All his actions therefore are coherent with making Malathi his - whether it is paying attention to his clothes and hair, writing letters to her or even asking his parents to get him married to her. There is no peace in his life and the turmoil of Chandran, embedded in the *Rajas Guna* of action with an ambition to marry Malathi has been narrated wonderfully by Narayan. He writes:

> The next day he showed with great care and paid a great deal of attention to his hair and awaited the evening. When evening came he put on his chocolate-coloured tweed coat and started out. At five, he was on the river bank, squatting on the sand near the spot where he had seen the girl the previous day. He sat there for over two hours. The girl did not come. Dozens of other towns people came to the river and sprawled all over the place, but not that girl. Chandran rose and walked along, peering furtively at every group. It was a very keen search, but it brought forth nothing. Why wasn't she there? His heart beat fast at the sight of every figure that approached the river clad in a *sari.* It was seven-forty-five when he set his face homeward, feeling that his brilliantine, shave, ironed tweed coat, were all wasted (56-57).

Malathi gets married to another man due to non-compability of their (Chandran's and Malathi's) horoscopes. Chandran gets dejected. The *Rajas Guna* of action impacts the man protagonist yet again and he leaves for Madras. Chandran tries to become a sanyasi by shaving his head, dying his clothes in ochre. His renunciation of the world is not to attain peace or solace, but in fact it is a revenge on society, parents, circumstances and fate which, he feels, is responsible for not getting the love of his life, Malathi.

The final part of the novel appears to involve another distinctive shift, back in Malgudi. Chandran is persuaded by his poet friend, Mohan, to try to become an agent for the Madras-based newspaper, *The Massenger*. Another visit to Madras helps him to secure this position, thanks to the mediation of his uncle. Chandran sets about devising strategies for increasing the newspaper's Malgudi circulation. In many ways this is the most important *Rajas Guna* 'action' shift in the novel, as it has Chandran metamorphosed from aimless drifter and romantic idealist into a practical businessman.

In the novel, *The Talkative Man*, the real story-teller is Narayan himself who uses Talkative Man as the representative of his own narrative medium. The entire novel highlights the *Rajas Guna* of action (non-stop talking is a primary mode of action) from the very first page when The Talkative Man says:

> They call me Talkative Man. Some affectionately shorten it to TM: I have earned this title, I suppose, because I cannot contain myself. My impulse to share an experience with others is irresistible, even if they sneer at my back. I don't care. I'd choke if I did not talk.... (1)

Throughout the novel, The Talkative Man, tells the story of Dr Rann interspersed by his own story where 'action' dominates the narrative:

> Still, I was busy from morning till night, moving about on my bicycle or on my neighbour Sambu's scooter. I was to be seen here and there, at municipal meetings, magistrates' court, the prize distribution at Albert Mission, with a reporter's notebook in hand and a fountain pen peeping out of my shirt pocket. I reported all kinds of activities, covering several kilometres a day on my vehicle and ended up at the railway station to post my despatch in the mail van with a late fee.... (3).

The Talkative Man admits that he 'liked to be active' (4). He is witty and has a sense of humour. When Dr Rann says that he was in Malgudi on a United Nations project, the Talkative Man says:

> ……Project is a self-contained phrase and may or may not be capable of elaboration. I come across the word in newspapers and among academicians, engineers and adventurers. One might hear the word and keep quiet, no probing further. Sometimes a project might involve nothing more than swatting flies and sending reports to the headquarters (9-10).

The *Rajas Guna* of action, makes the Talkative Man help Dr Rann, a complete stranger, in finding a house. He does get frustrated at Dr Rann's idiosyncrasies and cries out:

> Not a small house, nor a medium-sized one, not on the East or West, North or South, neither downtown or uptown…… (25).

The *Rajas Guna* of action coupled with the ambition to see his name in print drives him to take a picture of Dr Rann, the Timbactoo man, without his knowledge or consent. The Talkative Man is helped in this task by his friend Jayraj. He justifies it by saying that it 'was urgent and could be a turning point in (his) career' (31). The Talkative Man instigates Jayraj by saying:

> Be a good chap. My whole career depends on your help now. I'll manage to bring that man this way and you must manage to snap him, front or side, without his knowledge and enlarge it. We want only a bust (34).

The novel proceeds and the Talkative Man finds himself at crossroads. A woman arrives in Malgudi after seeing Dr Rann's picture in the weekly. She claims to be Dr Rann's wife and wants to be taken to him. However, Dr Rann says he doesn't wish to be disturbed. Further, he insists he has no wife. After several 'talking sessions' between the lady and Dr Rann she leaves for Delhi. The Talkative Man, despite his constant talk, is shown by Narayan, to have a sensitive trait. On realising that Dr Rann is eyeing the young granddaughter of the Town Hall Librarian he wants to 'puncture' him (77). He wants to cry out: Keep away, you- I don't know what to call you! She is young enough to be your daughter. You are a lecherous demon and wouldn't mind even if it were a grand-daughter! Keep off! (79). The *Rajas Guna* of action makes him spy on Dr Rann.

He says to himself:

> I bottled up my uneasiness at these reports. I had no clear notion what I could do about the situation or why. It was not my business, I said to myself, but then I began to have suspicions about Rann's background. Before tackling him, I wanted to arm myself with facts. I had no other recourse but to act as a spy. These days he went out after breakfast and kept away till lunch, came in the went out again. I realised that his movements were based on Girija's timetable. When he left in the afternoon, I could count on his absence all evening till eight o' clock or longer. I opened his room with a duplicate key. When I stepped in I felt like a burglar in my own home. I felt excited and hard pressed for time. I quickly examined his briefcase and a portfolio of letters- quite a handful. Envelopes addressed to different names only two to Rann- and the address was always Poste Restante in different towns and countries. Like our gods, he seemed to have a thousand names- Ashok, Naren, D'Cruz, John, Adam, Shankar, Sridhar, Singh, Iqbal and what not. The letters were all from women imploring appealing and accusing and attacking in a forthright manner… (85-6).

The *Rajas Guna* of action, activity and movement dominates the man protagonist Madhu's (his name is revealed much later by Narayan in the novel) life. Lying in bed he keeps 'sifting and analysing and finding justifications and overcoming doubts and suspicions about Girija and Rann' (93) till he falls asleep well past midnight. When Madhu gets to know from Gaffur, the taxi-driver, that Dr Rann was planning to elope with Girija, he hatches a plan:

> I had to avoid upsetting anyone on any side. The old librarian must be protected from shock or a stroke, Girija from a public scandal and an eventual desertion in some far-off place and all the frustration and tragedy that befell every woman captivated by Rann's charms. My mind wandered over morbid details as to how far the girl had admitted him; when it was all over one must somehow take her to Dr Lazarus, the lady doctor at the Government Hospital, to get her examined for a possible abortion, a better evil than being burdened with a fatherless child. While the other women in Rann's life were perhaps hardy and sophisticated, capable of

withstanding the tragedy, this girl was innocent, her mind in a nascent state, unless already complicated and corrupted by association with Rann (97).

In sync with his plan, Madhu sends a telegram to Commandant Sarasa, the same lady who was in Malgudi earlier and had claimed to be Dr Rann's wife. It reads:

> COME IMMEDIATELY. YOUR HUSBAND FOUND. COME BEFORE HE IS LOST AGAIN. YOUR ONLY FINAL CHANCE TO ROPE HIM. STAY RAILWAY WAITING ROOM. I'VE FIXED IT. TAKE CARE NOT TO BE SEEN IN TOWN. WILL MEET AND EXPLAIN FURTHER PROCEDURE (98).

Madhu succeeds in his act of timely intervention (totally embedded) in the *Rajas Guna* of activity with an ambition to save Girija). He foils Dr Rann's plan of eloping with Girija. Thus, R.K. Narayan, the master story-teller, is able to highlight the *Rajas Guna* of action and ambition in the personality of *The Talkative Man.*

The man protagonist Mr. Sampath a printer by profession, in the novel by the same name is introduced to the readers while he is immersed in the activity of printing. The *Rajas Guna* of action not only dominates his disposition, but also his work. A printing machine is symbolic of the *Rajas Guna* of action as it is constantly running-day in and day out, printing material for clients. While working in his press *Truth Printing Works*, Mr. Sampath dresses in Khaki shorts and explains:

> The best dress for my type of work. I am going on the machine to-day. You see, I solve the labour problem by not being a slave to my workmen. When it comes to a pinch, I can do every bit of work myself, including gumming and pasting (21).

The man protagonist is heavily under the influence of *Rajas Guna* of activity. He spends 'four nights and days' (18 - 21) designing a layout for Srinivas 'Weekly, *The Banner*'. He has a way with words and impresses his client, Srinivas. A true businessman, the printer woos Srinivas when he says: 'When a customer enters our premises he is, in our view, a guest of Truth Printing Works. Well, you think, *The Banner* is yours. It isn't. I view it as my own' (21). Highlighting Mr Sampath's *Rajas Guna* Narayan writes of him:

> He acted up to this principle. In the weeks preceding the launching of *The Banner* he abandoned all his normal work: he set aside a co-operative society balance sheet, four wedding invitations and a small volume of verse, all of which were urgent, according to those who had ordered them. He dealt with all his customers amiably, but to no purpose, "You will get the proofs positively this evening and tomorrow you may come for the finished copies. Sorry for the delay. My staff is somewhat overworked at the moment. They've instructions to give you the maximum co-operation." With all this suaveness he was not to be found in his place at the appointed hour. He threw a scarf around his throat, donned a fur cup and was out on one or the other duties connected with *The Banner* (21).

Although Narayan introduces the printer early in the novel, the fact that he is Mr. Sampath - the man protagonist is revealed only on page 67 after a short flash back. The printer reasserts that 'when a person becomes my customer, he becomes a sort of blood relation of mine' (68). Mr. Sampath is shown to be a busy man printing speeches for important people in town. However, due to labour problems in the printing office *The Banner* has to discontinue. This leaves Srinivas upset. The man protagonist reassures him. He says:

> It is my duty to see that *The Banner* is out again. Please wait. I will see that the journal is set up on a lino machine and printed off a rotary and dispatched in truck-loads every week. For this we need a lot of money. Don't you doubt it for a moment. I am going to make a lot of money, ... (89).

Mr. Sampath is a married man with five children. Narayan portrays him as being sensitive to his children's needs. The *Rajas Guna* of activity and movement is predominating in his domestic life. The man protagonist is shown to be actively involved in activities of his children. He teaches them how to dance while he himself plays 'on his harmonium' (88).

In order to make more money, Mr. Sampath gets 'interested in films' (89). He encourages Srinivas to also go and see the film studio. They are travelling by bus when the conductor asks him if his printing press is not working. He lies and says easily: "Old machines they are worn out" (90). Although Mr. Sampath ropes in Srinivas as a story writer into the *Sunrise Pictures*, the *Rajas Guna* of action and ambition to make quick money makes him dismiss Srinivas' ideas. Srinivas' story on *Gandhian* philosophy for the motion picture is brushed aside as is his suggestion of *Krishna- Leela, Hanumaan, Draupadi, Garuda* and so on. His argument is:

> After we have made three or four films we shall perhaps gain confidence enough to take up a subject like yours, but now we have to move on safe ground (99).

When Somu suggests *The Burning to Ashes of Kama- God of love* (100), Mr. Sampath is happy and his stand on it is that no one had attempted the subject earlier. Mr. Somu then narrates the story 'humming and hawing and clearing his throat' (100). After finalising the script, Sampath plans to get rupees fifty thousand to produce the picture. He says:

> I must find fifty thousand rupees if I have to produce the picture. This will enable me to go through the picture with a free and independent mind and when it is done, or rather, even when we are halfway through it, we can realise the entire amount and more by selling the territorial rights for distributors (114).

For this he persuades Srinivas to speak to his landlord to invest money in the picture. Narayan's skill as a writer makes it known to the readers later, how Sampath, immersed in the *Rajas Guna* of ambition uses the old landlord to get the loan on the pretext of learning the religious scripts and also arranging marriage for the landlord's grand-daughter.

After the landlord's sudden death, the *Rajas Guna* of activity makes Sampath tell lies. The man protagonist is shown by Narayan to use other people for his selfish reasons and monetary gains. To suit his purpose, Sampath can go to any extent. He is not truthful to the landlord when he wants his money and neither is he truthful to the investigating authorities after the landlord's death. Narayan writes:

> They summoned Sampath because he was often seen going there. He looked panicky, as if they were going to haul him up for murder.

> A statement from him was recorded as to why he visited the old man so often. He explained that he was his student and was learning Sanskrit from him. And then they set out a number of exhibits- a saving bank passbook, a piece of paper on which were scrawled 12½ percent, 5,000 and the name Sampath. He was asked if had seen the passbook before. Sampath said, "No". He was asked to explain what he knew about the piece of paper containing his name and the 12½ percent calculation. He said that he was consulted by the old man regarding some investment calculation and possibly he had tried to work it out. The Panchayatdars pried further and wanted to know what the investment was. Sampath who had by now recovered something of his composure, answered: "How should I know? Occasionally my master would talk of investments generally and work out hypothetically some figures. I don't know what he had in mind (149-50).

The story proceeds and the movie gets started. Later, when the hero of the movie wants more money, Sampath gets him thrown out of the studio. Instead, he takes on the role of Shiva, the hero, himself. He holds that 'no one is indispensable in this world' (185). He says:

> We need not be at the mercy of these mercenaries. I will do Shiva myself. I've been an actor once. We've bothered our heads with it for four days. I always felt that we might do it ourselves, save all trouble instead of trying to teach it to these fools. What do you say, Dance Master (184-5).

Lust and greed coupled with ambition makes Sampath tread the path of frenzied 'action' where from becoming the producer, he changes to the main lead actor portraying the role of Shiva with the woman protagonist, Shanti, as Parvathi. He gets romantically involved with Shanti. Throughout the novel, the *Rajas Guna* of action, activity and ambition to earn more money dominates the man protagonist, Sampath. Events take a turn. His projects fail and yet, his spirit does not. He is still hopeful to get a new project started. This overwhelming trait of ambition, lies and frenzied activity portrayed by Narayan in the character of Mr. Sampath agitates Srinivas so much that at the end of the novel, he is happy to bid Mr. Sampath goodbye forever.

The setting of R.K. Narayan's novel, *The Guide*, as in most of his novels, is Malgudi, a fictional town in Southern India. The novel is told through a series of flash blacks in which the man protagonist is totally under the influence of the *Rajas Guna* of action and ambition. In fact, this novel brings out the *Rajas Guna* of action and ambition with a clarity which is the forte of Narayan. *The Guide* opens with Raju as the central character. It intertwines two narratives- one, of the protagonist, recounting in first person his own life's story. The other, the narrator describing the protagonist's story. The *Rajas Guna* of action so impacts Raju that he 'feels like an actor who was always expected to utter the right sentence' (14). He grows up near a railway station, becomes a resourceful tourist guide. He meets Rosie, a beautiful dancer and her anthropologist husband, Marco. Raju gets attracted to Rosie and while Marco is away studying cave paintings, he lures her into a relationship with himself. Marco finds about his wife's affair, leaves Rosie and goes away to Madras. The 'action' driven Raju combined with the *Rajas Guna* of 'ambition' takes upon himself to make Rosie into a great dancer. He promises her:

> You are in the right place. Forget all your past. We will teach that cad a lesson by and by… First, I'll make the world recognise you as the greatest artist of the time (153).

Despite Rosie being a married woman and despite Raju's mother objecting to letting her stay, he allows Rosie to live in his own house. Rosie stays and starts to practice her dance regularly. Under the spell of *Rajas Guna*, nothing matters to Raju anymore. Neither his reputation of living with a married woman, nor his suffering work as a tourist guide. By and by the finances become low and Raju is unable to pay his creditor for 'months and months' (159). 'Living with Rosie under the same roof is enough' (161) for him. He wants 'nothing more in life' and the 'world outside Rosie' (161) seems unreal to him. Raju says to his friend Gaffur:

> ……'if I had five hundred rupees. I could start a new life……She is a gold-mine……If I had money to start her with- oh!'…You know *Bharat Natvam* is really the greatest art business today. There is such a craze today that people will pay anything to see the best.
>
> I can not do anything about it because I have no money. Can't you help me, Gaffur? (162).

Rosie's dance practices continue. Raju finds a new stage name for her. He wants the world to know her as 'Nalini'. Opportunity strikes when the *Albert Mission* boys are about to have their annual social. Raju suggests to the committee members: 'Why not a dance recital instead of the usual Shakespeare tragedy?'(177). He encourages them to go with him and see the 'sample of the show'(178). When the members like Rosie's performance, the *Rajas Guna* of action and ambition makes Raju bargain for 'drummer and accompanists…Rosie had been clamouring for all along' (181).

There is no turning back for Rosie. Her talent for dance combined with the initial push by Raju, makes her career soar and her name becomes 'public property' (182). The *Rajas Guna* of action makes Raju take all the credit for her success. He says to himself:

> At that time I was puffed up with the thought of how I had made her..........at the time there was no limit to my self-congratulation. When I watched her in a large hall with a thousand eyes focused on her, I had no doubt that people were telling themselves and each other, 'there he is, the man but for whom –' And I imagined all this adulation lapping around my ears like wavelets. In every show I took, as a matter of right, the middle sofa in the first row. I gave it out that that was my seat wherever I might go and unless I sat there Nalini would be unable to perform. She needed my inspiring presence. I shook my head discreetly; sometimes I lightly tapped my fingers together in timing. When I met her eyes, I smiled familiarly at her on the stage. Sometimes I signalled her a message with my eyes and fingers, suggesting a modification or a criticism of her performance (182).

And further:

> I really liked to parade her through the gaping crowds. After the show, there were still people hanging around to catch a glimpse of the star. I walked ahead of her or beside her without much concern. At the end of the performance they presented her with a large garland of flowers and they gave me one too. I accepted mine with protest. 'There is really no reason why you should waste money on a garland for me,' I said; I slung it carelessly on my arm or in the thick of the crowd dramatically handed it over the

Nalini with 'Well, you really deserve two,' and made her carry it for me (184).

Raju's ambition of earning money comes true. With Nalini's success he starts to demand the highest fee and gets it. He treats those that come to ask for 'a show as supplicants' (194). He has a massive monthly income and spends 'an enormous amount on servants and style' (194). Raju pays an immense amount on income tax. The *Rajas Guna* of activity and action coupled with the ambition of getting more and more money drives Raju into a frenzy. Narayan sums up Raju's personality heavily affected by the *Rajas Guna* when he makes Raju question Nalini, 'Well you have a big household, a big car and what not- is that not enjoyment of life?' (194). Narayan aptly writes of Raju:

> It seemed absurd that we should earn less than the maximum we could manage. My philosophy was that while it lasted, the maximum money had to be squeezed out. We needed all the money in the world. If I were less prosperous, who would care for me? Where would be the smiles which greeted me now wherever I turned and the respectful agreement shown to my remarks when I said something to the man in the next chair? It filled me with dread that I should be expected to do with less. 'If we don't work and earn when the time is good, we commit a sin. When we have a bad time no one will help us.' I was planning big investments as soon as possible- as soon as we could count on a little more margin. As it was, the style of living and entertaining which I had evolved was eating up all our resources (195).

The ambition of getting more money and also the insecurity of losing Rosie to her husband, Marco, drives Raju to a point of forging Rosie's signature for a package of jewels. This lands him a two-year prison sentence. Narayan with his skill has crafted Raju's character with such elan that even as a prisoner, the *Rajas Guna* of action predominates his disposition. Raju in his own words is 'considered a model prisoner' and a 'master of the show' (226). He 'visited all departments of the prison as a sort of benevolent supervisor' (226). Raju says:

> I got on well with all the warders: I relieved them in their jobs when other prisoners had to be watched. I watched the weaving

> section and the carpentry sheds. Whether they were murderers of cut-throats or highwaymen, they all listened to me, and I could talk them out of their blackest moods. When there was respite, I told them stories and philosophies and what not. They came to refer to me as *Vadhyar*-that is, Teacher... when the jail superintendent went about his inspections, I was one of those privileged to walk behind and listen to his remarks; and I ran little errands for him, which endeared me to him. He had only to look ever so slightly to his left, and I knew what he wanted. I dashed up and called the warder he was thinking of calling; he had only to hesitate for a second and I knew he wanted the pebble on the road to be picked up and thrown away......I worked incessantly on a vegetable patch in the backyard of the superintendent's home. I dug the earth and drew water from the well and tended it carefully. I put fences round, with brambles and thorns so that cattle did not destroy the plants. I grew huge *brinjals* and beans, and cabbages. When they appeared on their stalks as tiny buds, I was filled with excitement. I watched them develop, acquire shape, change colour, shed the early parts.... (226-7).

Raju is deeply hurt to find out that while he is in jail, Nalini goes on with her successful dance shows and finally leaves Madras for good. On his release from prison, Raju stops to rest near an abandoned temple, where a villager named Velan mistakes him for a holy man. Since Raju doesn't want to disgrace his friends in Malgudi, he decides to stay on and 'act' as the holyman. In bargain, he is happy to accept the daily offering of food which the villagers bring him. Events take a turn and a drought in the village leads him to take on a twelve day fast. The *Rajas Guna* of action impacts his personality so much that he takes this fast very seriously. The ambition, this time is neither love nor money, but being true to the belief of villagers and the hope for rain. The novel ends with the starved Raju becoming weak and collapsing while it is seen raining upon the hills. The entire novel, thus, has been written by Narayan where he has superbly crafted the man protagonist embedded in traits highlighting the dominant *Rajas Guna.*

Ambition and Action dominate the above men protagonists and their personalities are shaped by this trait of *Rajas Guna.*

Thus, the men protagonists in the above novels, **Swaminathan** in *Swami and Friends*, **Chandran** in *The Bachelor of Arts*, **Krishna** in *The English Teacher*, **Sampath** in *Mr. Sampath*, **Raju** in *The Guide* and **Madhu** in *A Talkative Man* display characteristics of *Rajas Guna.* Their personalities show the effect of desire, passion and lust. Their disposition reflects their attachment to people and things. Their obedience to the commands of preceptors and parents is embedded in the wish to please irrespective of the command being right or wrong. Their focus on 'action' is because of personal gain as a consequence. Finally, ambition to succeed in the journey of life is what governs their thinking and thus their doing.

4

Influence of *Tamas Guna*

Novels and Characters

R.K. Narayan writes of India, it's people, culture and relationships. Though none of his man protagonists can be called 'villians' in the strict definition of the word, predominant traits of delusion, jealousy, anger and absence of self-control are prevalent in the personality of Narayan's characters. These then, qualify such characters, to be clubbed under the impact of *Tamas Guna.* The predominance of *Sattva, Rajas* or *Tamas Guna* are seen in various facets of characters where *Tamas* is the lowest of the three. *Tamas* is a force which promotes darkness, dissolution, death, destruction, ignorance, sloth and resistance. Tamas is dull, insensible, gloomy and dark energy. The Sanskrit translation of the word means 'darkness, dark-blue, black'. People under the impact of this *Guna* are gloomy, lazy, dull and blinded by greed. Sometimes people who are *Tamasic* can be characterised as lazy and slothful. On the darker end of the *Tamasic* scale, they can be unconscious of the needs of others, dark and destructive. Food which is *Tamasic* is stale, under-ripe or over-ripe, canned, reheated or fermented. Eating too much is *Tamasic. Tamas* (Sanskrit for 'darkness', 'obscurity') has been translated to mean too inactive, negative, lethargic, dull, or slow. *Tamas* has also been translated as indifference, the most negative quality because it is the rejection of *Karmic* Law. The central principle of *Dharma* in Hinduism is that one's *Karma* (action) must be worked out and not ignored.

In Hindu mythology, *Tamas* is also a *Guna* or quality which is much needed to counter the Evil, for example, *Bhairava,* the incarnation of Lord Shiva, is a Tamasic Avatar and Lord Shiva Himself out of the Trinity represents *Tamas*, where Shiva drinks the poison of his devotees to get rid of their sins, hence absorbing the *Tamo-Guna* of devotees.

Chapter 14 of *Bhagvad Gita* states:

> ......And know Tamas to be born of ignorance, stupefying all embodied beings; it binds fast, O descendant of Bharata, by miscomprehension, indolence and darkness, inertness, miscomprehension and delusion, —these arise when Tamas is predominant. The fruit of good action, they say, is Sattva, the fruit of Rajas is pain and ignorance is the fruit of Tamas. From Sattva arises wisdom and greed from Rajas; miscomprehension, delusion and ignorance arise from Tamas. The embodied one having gone beyond these three Gunas out of which the body is evolved, is freed from birth, death, decay and pain and attains to immortality.

Tamas has two basic characteristics: *Gurutva* (magnetic pull) and *Avarnaka* (the capacity of covering or concealing). Due to the *Gurutva* quality, it dominates over *Rajas* and *Sattva Gunas*. The third characteristic or the result of *Tamas Guna* is *Visada* which refers to ignorance, delusion and depression.

Narayan in his novels ***The Dark Room* (1938), *The Financial Expert* (1952), *The World of Nagaraj* (1990) and *The Grandmother's Tale* (1992)** creates a storyline where the predominance of *Tamas Guna* gets reflected in the men protagonists.

Ramani in *The Dark Room*

Margayya in *The Financial Expert*

Nagaraj in *The World of Nagaraj*

Viswanath in *Grandmother's Tale* are men protagonists who show qualities of complete delusion, ignorance, indecision with respect to action, greed, censure of good acts, rashness of judgment, crookedness, sinful action and absence of self-control. Thus, they show the impact of *Tamas Guna*. To study and understand the impact of *Tamas Guna* on the man protagonists in Narayan's novels, the chief three characteristics prevalent under this *Guna* are undertaken:

(a) Lack of Self-control

(b) Delusion

(c) Ignorance

The Dark Room (1938) is the story of Ramani, the Branch Manager of the *Engladia Insurance Company* and his wife Savitri. Ramani and Savitri are married with three children Babu, Kamala and Sumati.

Narayan sketches their married life and writes about Savitri who gets upset occasionally by Ramani's behaviour. She finds solace when she is alone sulking in the dark room, 'a musty unlit store-room' next to the kitchen. Even though Ramani is aware of her hurt when she lies lonely in the dark room, he remains indifferent towards her. Later in the novel, Narayan introduces the character of Shanta Bai as a Probationary Insurance Assistant who joins Ramani's office. Events take a turn and Ramani's lack of self-control leads him to woo Shanta Bai and to have an affair with her. When Savitri comes to know about their affair she tries to intervene and put a stop to their relationship. Ramani refuses to do so. Savitri leaves the house to end her life. However, this does not happen and she is saved by a low caste blacksmith Mari. He and his wife Ponni take care of Savitri but after a few days of hardship and loneliness she returns to her home and children.

R.K. Narayan's novel *The Financial Expert* (1952) tells the story of the rise and fall of the man protagonist Margayya. He is shown to be a petty money-lender sitting under a Banyan tree, across the Central Co-operative Land Mortgage Bank, in the town of Malgudi. Story progresses and Balu, Margayya's little son, throws his account book into a gutter. It then becomes impossible for Margayya to resume his old practice. The man protagonist is in need of money and on the behest of an astrologer, offers prayers to *Lakshmi,* the Goddess of Wealth, for forty days. The character of Dr Pal is introduced by Narayan in the novel who sells Margayya the manuscript of a book named *Domestic Harmony*. Madan Lal, a publisher publishes the book which becomes popular in a big way making Margayya very rich. The story unfolds and Balu runs away from home. Days pass and Margayya receives a letter saying Balu is dead. Margayya leaves for Madras, discovers through a police inspector that his son is not really dead, traces the boy and brings him home. Margayya gets Balu married. Margayya meets Dr Pal again and the two, through a deal, make great profits. However, Balu gets into wrong company and along with Dr Pal starts to spend his time gambling and womanising. Margayya gets into a fight with Dr Pal who in turn ruins Margayya's business. All the accumulated wealth is disbursed and the man protagonist goes back to his old job of lending money under the old banyan tree.

The World of Nagaraj (1990), by R.K. Narayan is the story of man protagonist, Nagaraj who fancies himself as a man with a mission. Nagaraj does not fully understand the nature of this mission, even though he expends considerable energy pursuing it. His main purpose, he believes, is to write a biography of the mythological character Narada - the celestial sage. Nagaraj is neither sure of this subject, nor does he pursue his ambition with vigour. His daily activities consist of meditating in his ochre robe which some Guru has given him, wandering in the market place and chatting with neighbours. His favourite pastime is sitting in his verandah and day-dreaming! His elder brother Gopu and wife, Charu, live in a different village with their son Tim. Life for Nagaraj takes a turn when Tim, his nephew, comes to live with him in Malgudi. Initially Nagaraj and his wife, Sita, are thrilled to have Tim over. However, later they are worried since Tim secretly leaves college, takes to drinking and visits *kismet*, a night-club. Narayan through his skills brings out the *Tamas Guna* of delusion in Nagaraj where he takes no action throughout the course of the novel. Whether it is engaging in a conversation with his brother, correcting Tim for his activities or embarking on the project on Narada, Nagaraj fails at everything.

The novel *Grandmother's Tale* (1992), is the story of Narayan's great-grandmother, Bala. Narayan writes how she taught him to recite a Sanskrit lyric every day. The Sanskrit lyric stated that the perfect woman is she who works like a slave, looks like a goddess, gives advice like a minister, has patience like Mother Earth and is 'courtesan-like' in the bed-chamber. Narayan tells the readers how his great-grandmother is married as a child and how her husband leaves her shortly after. The priestly traditions, back then, forbade a child bride from visiting the temple unless her husband was found alive. Bala then sets out on a journey to find her missing husband. After years of searching, she finds him in Poona, rich and thriving, as a jewellery-business owner. Enraged by the fact that he has got married again, she gets rid of his second wife. The man protagonist Vishwanath is under the impact of *Tamas Guna* of lack of self-control. He gets so blinded by comforts that he gets married outside of his already existing marriage to Bala.

The central men characters in the above novels, **Ramani** in *The Dark Room*, **Margayya** in *The Financial Expert*, **Nagaraj** in *The World of Nagaraj* and **Vishwanath** in *Grandmother's Tale* are delusionary, lazy, ignorant and have no control over their actions, thoughts and words. Thus, they all come in the domain of *Tamas Guna*.

Lack of Self-control

Lack of self-control is the inability to control one's emotions and behaviour. The desires in the face of external demands overpower the personality of a being in such a way that there is no self-regulation. This trait of lack of self-control comes under the *Tamas Guna* because it disables the achievement of goals. There is a tendency to react on the impulse where a barrage of emotions overwhelms a person's disposition.

R.K. Narayan, in his novel, *The Dark Room,* has portrayed the character of the man protagonist Ramani in shades which qualify him under the highlighting *Tamas Guna*. Ramani's lack of self-control leads him to have an affair outside of his marriage. This hurts his wife. His complete disregard for self-control compels her to leave him. Ramani's character is sketched by Narayan as a *flat* character as it does not undergo any substantial change or growth in the course of the story. Referred to as a two-dimensional character or static character in the work of fiction, Ramani's flat character does not show progress in the development of emotions or relationships. Chauvinism, dominance, lack of empathy and controlling behaviour can broadly be clubbed under the umbrella of 'lack of self-control'. Narayan brings out these shades in the personality of Ramani qualifying him under the dominance of *Tamas Guna*. The novel begins with Narayan showing the man protagonist Ramani drenched in male chauvinism. He is rude to his wife Savitri and tells her (when she defends their son's absence from school) to 'Go and do any work you like in the kitchen, but leave the training of a grown-up boy to me. It is none of a woman's business' (1).

Ramani has no control on his words. When he does not like the food Savitri serves him, he complains:

> Brinjals, cucumber, radish and greens, all the twelve months in the year and all the thirty days in the month. I don't know when I shall have a little decent food to eat. I slave all day in the office for this mouthful. No lack of expenses, money for this and money for that. If the cook can't cook properly, do the work yourself. What have you to do better than that? (2).

So rude and overpowering is Ramani that Savitri gets intimidated by him. R.K. Narayan writes:

> Savitri hovered between the cook and her husband, watching every item on his dining-leaf and instructing the cook to bring a second or a third helping. This was by no means an easy task, for Ramani was eccentric and lawless in his taste. "Why do you torment me with this cucumber for the dozenth time? Do you think I live on it?" or he would say, if there was the slightest delay, "Ah, ah! I suppose I'll have to apply to my office for leave and wait for this salted cucumber! A fine thing. Never knew people could be so niggardly with cucumber, the cheapest trash in the market" (2).

When Savitri refuses to interrupt him, her silence infuriates Ramani. He says, 'Saving up your energy by being silent! Saving it up for the purpose? When a man asks you something you could do worse than honour him with a reply' (3) . On the other hand, when she offers an explanation, as occasionally happened, she is told , 'shut up'. Words won't mend a piece of foul cooking (3). Ramani's *Tamas Guna* of lack of self-control is seen in his words, actions and thoughts. It is limited not only to his behaviour towards his wife, but in all his relationships. Narayan writes:

> While dressing up for his office Ramani would keep calling the servant Ranga in order to tell him what he was and where he ought to be for not polishing the boots properly, for folding the trousers with a wrong crease, for leaving the coat on the frame with all the

pockets bulging out. Savitri, too, would sometimes be told what her husband thought of her for not attending to buttons or sock-holes and for not keeping an eye on Ranga' (3).

Throughout the novel, Ramani's character shows lack of self-control. This *Tamas Guna* precipitates into soft undertones of charm, when he tries to woo the other woman, Shanta Bai, a new assistant in his office. He is inconsiderate towards his wife, but just because he wants Shanta Bai's attention, he is polite and charming. When Shanta Bai asks him to sit down, he says, '.... not when a lady is standing' (62). There is a marked difference in his choice of words and behaviour pattern, which Narayan gives his protagonist when he is with his wife vis-à-vis when he is with Shanta Bai. Ramani gives Shanta Bai his undivided attention and says, 'men deserve to be whipped' when she hints at a couple of attempts on her honour' (63). Ramani's character infuses charm and humour when he wants to flirt with and impress Shanta Bai. On her insistence at taking the back seat in the car, Ramani says, 'but the engine won't start unless there are two passengers in the front seat' (65).

Sarbani Putatunda interprets Ramani thus:

> [.....] Ramani's arrogance plainly blinds him from admitting even to himself his offence- adultery. The concept, in fact, never crosses his mind. Liaison with a woman other than his wife is just a pastime for him and hence, he can not comprehend Savitri's violent reaction against it. Savitri is right in pointing out that women are but playthings to him to be fondled and kicked when he chose. As the saying goes, 'the devil quotes the scriptures,' Ramani too attempts self-justification by quoting scriptures. A wife's primary duty, he observes, is to tolerate everything her husband does. No matter how wayward he is, she has no right to censor him. Wifely duty demands complete subservience and Savitri, according to Ramani, has flouted this decorum (74).

The man protagonist's selfishness shines when he gives the favourite bench of his wife for Shanta Bai's room. Further, when Savitri comes to know of his affair with Shanta Bai and wants to leave the house along with the children, Ramani is least ashamed of his acts. Albeit, he tells Savitri to leave the house but not to 'touch' the children or 'talk to them' as he clearly states 'they are my children' (88) and that '(T) hey will get on splendidly without you, don't you worry. No one is indispensable in this world' (88). When the children ask Ramani about their mother, he lies to them, saying she has gone to see their unwell grandfather. This is because he does not have the courage to tell them that it was because of his own relationship with the other woman that Savitri was hurt and thus left home. Two days pass and she does not return. Portraying Ramani's selfish behaviour, when his son questions him about Savitri, Narayan writes:

> Ramani was slightly frightened. He himself had not been quite easy in mind since the morning. It was three days since she left and still there was no sign of her. While the Strong Man in him said that she couldn't have gone far and that she was bound to return when she regained sense, the Weak Man, so long unnoticed by himself, constantly pricked him with the reminder that she had been gone two days and three nights now; and suppose she had done something very rash and foolish or something had happened to her, how was he to answer the children, her people and everybody? People would talk: "This wife of the Secretary of the Engladia Insurance Company…He shuddered. If anything happened he would have to pack out of Malgudi…." (185).

This behaviour is not so much for the state of Savitri, as is for his own reputation. He thinks 'People would talk. The wife of the secretary…..'. The discomfort of looking for his lost wife makes him hate himself. He 'hated Savitri for bringing him to this pass and he hated Babu, his son for disturbing his peace (157). He still gives in to the pleasures of the flesh as he 'drives into race course and stops before his office to meet Shanta Bai'.

The novel ends with Savitri returning home. However, the character of Ramani stays typically conventional. He still goes about his normal routine of dressing up and going to the office (159). He pretends that nothing has changed and gets jasmine for Savitri to please her 'looking at her mischievously' (160). He tries to humour her without addressing issues about her mental state. He goes to sleep and neither does he enter into any conversation nor tries to understand the reason behind his wife's indifference when she says, 'I am very tired. I must sleep' (161). S. R. Ramteke studying R. K. Narayan and his social perspective observes of *The Dark Room*:

> It is Manu and the later moralists who have made the woman what she is today, weak and utterly helpless. That a woman should have no freedom, is so deeply imbedded in the minds of both Ramani and Savitri, that Ramani could bluntly tell her that she has no right whatsoever over the children. Savitri could not question him....; she appears to be only a weak, whimpering, timid, spineless and vacillating character. Her plight fails to evoke even pathos, for she is shown to be a bundle of changing moods and conflicting responses. Savitri's pathetic utterances show how miserable she is in her married life. 'I don't possess anything in this world.
>
> What possession can a woman call her own except her body? Everything else that she has is her father's, her husband' or her son's' (13).

The culmination of the story has Savitri choosing to live with Ramani, even though she feels that a part of her 'is dead'. (160) The title of the novel *The Dark Room* signifies the room, next to the store room where Savitri retires whenever she is overwhelmed by emotions of hurt and anger (mainly at the hands of her husband). The dark room is synonymous with Savitri's emotions where she cries and lets out her feelings of frustration. The utter helplessness of a woman, in a conventional patriarchal society, who can not be an individual identity but only a daughter, a wife or a mother is brought out with tact by Narayan. It is this dark room which gives her solace, where she resolves her unhappy feelings and prepares herself again to live up to her image of a wife and mother. The man protagonist Ramani is heavily under the influence of *Tamas Guna* of lack of self-control. This has been portrayed wonderfully by R.K. Narayan.

The story in the novel *Grandmother's Tale* sees the ten years old man protagonist Viswanath marrying the seven-year-old Bala. Though at the beginning of the novel, the protagonist is a child, his character, when traced in the course of the story, is impacted by the *Tamas Guna* of lack of self-control. Viswanath gets so blinded by comforts that he gets married outside of his already existing marriage to Bala. After his marriage to Bala as a child, Viswanath, the bridegroom, goes back to his school run by a pedagogue on a brick platform under a Banyan tree on the riverside. He is 'ragged by his class-fellows for getting married' (13). Narayan portrays the plight of Viswanath, a victim of child-marriage. He writes:

> A few cried, "Shame, shame," which was the usual form of greeting in their society. The teacher tapped his cane on the floor and cried out over the tumult, "Why shame?" I was married when I was like Vishwa. I have four sons and two daughters and grandchildren (14).

Since Bala is only seven years old she has to wait until she attains puberty and then go through an elaborate nuptial ceremony before she can join her husband. Thus, Bala stays at her parent's house while Viswanath stays at his. Days pass and the naive man protagonist, in his ignorance of the seriousness of a man-wife relationship, leaves the town with some pilgrims. Of course, he does mention to his child-bride that he is leaving for Poona. The future and fate of Bala, his wife, who is left alone does not cross his mind. The storyline progresses and Bala attains maturity. Society's comments and several restrictions put on her by virtue of being without her husband, disturbs her. Bala decides to go on a woman-hunt for her missing husband. After many false starts, she gets on the right track and joins travellers going on foot or by some mode of transport and reaches 'Poona about a year later' (34). Here after many hurdles, she comes across a home where a woman agrees to feed her and gradually gives her shelter in her own house. By and by Bala learns that Surma, the woman's husband is none other but her own husband Viswanath. Narayan highlights the disposition of lack of self-control in Viswanath by writing that even though the protagonist is aware of his marriage to Bala, he still finds Surma, the rich heiress to a gem merchant and gets married to her. Surma tells Bala:

> My father did not approve of our proposal to marry at first. He threatened to throw him out not only from our shop but from this country itself and ordered me not to talk to him and confined me at home. I had a miserable time. We eloped to Nasik and were married in the temple of Triambaka – a sort of marriage, quiet and private. Eventually, father reconciled himself to the situation. When he died the gem business and the house fell to my share (49).

Bala manoeuvres and finds ways to lure her husband back. She reveals her identity to Viswa. On learning the facts, he is so distressed that he falls sick. Bala hatches a plan wherein she tells Surma to travel to the temples in South, specially to 'Gunasekaram where mental sickness is cured miraculously through offering and puja to that God' (58) to pray for good health of Viswa. On the other hand, she tells Viswa to let Surma stay back and not go for the trip so that they can travel back to their legitimate home. Viswa's lack of self-control is highlighted again in his actions towards Surma. Even though he is aware that Surma will commit suicide on hearing that Bala was his legal wife and that he also couldn't live without Surma, Viswanath does nothing. All three travel to the South where they spend time together.

On one occasion Bala steps into deep waters and asks Viswa to turn Surma back to Poona. She threatens to drown herself if her wish is not met with. The man protagonist heavily under the *Tamas Guna* of lack of self-control does not intervene or take the side of Surma. He stands there 'dumbstruck' (69). Surma is left alone to go back to Poona and Viswa returns to his hometown with Bala. Stressing on his thankless character, Narayan calls Viwanath a 'tramp' who is only a 'lowly clerk' in Surma's father's shop in the beginning and rises high 'mainly through Surma's support' (65).

Viswanath is portrayed by Narayan as a thankless man lacking in self-control. He comes back to his village, his appearance changed with his hair and beard cut but is unable to locate his house and parents. Narayan writes:

> Viswa had left the place thirty years and Bala about twenty years, before. Most of the landmarks were gone……Viswa searched for his old house but could not locate it. That neighbourhood had been demolished and he could not find anyone to answer his questions, expect a man grazing his cow, who just said, "Ask someone else. I know nothing." Viswa tried here and there, but could get no news of his parents or his relatives. The village seemed to have been deserted by all the old families. Bala's main purpose to visit the temple and offer puja to Ranganatha accomplished, she saw no reason for staying in the village. They decided to move a

near- by town where Viswa could established himself as a gem merchant and start a new life (70 - 71).

Vishwanath establishes himself as a gem expert in Kumbakonam. His reputation spreads as an expert appraiser of gems. People bring him diamonds for evaluation and to check for flaws. Through an eye glass he examines the stone and gives his verdict before they are handed over to the goldsmith for setting. Time passes by and they are blessed with four children- three daughters and a son. The next twenty years, roughly, are years of prosperity. Vishwa's business flourishes. In proper time, he finds bridegrooms for his daughters and sends his son to study in Madras at the Medical College. Vishwa is past sixty when he finds himself isolated, what with all his children married and well settled. When Viswa is nearing seventy he works less and less, gradually stopping all business. After Bala's death, Vishwanath is persuaded to go to Kolar with his son. Here too, as with his past relationships, troubles arise between Viswa, his son and the daughter-in-law. He fails to see the reasonable side of things and magnifies the problem, if any. He says about his children:

> He is becoming really indifferent. This morning he left without a word to me. All of them are behaving callously. Children get out and come in as they please. They don't notice me at all. Lakshmi thinks her duty is done after feeding me as she would feed a dog without a word. 'The last three days Swami never spoke to me more than three sentences. They think I am an orphan depending on their favours. This is the curse of old age. I will teach them a lesson (86-89).

So low is Viswanath's self-control that he does not wait for his son to come back from work. Neither does he inform his daughter-in-law of his whereabouts. Rather, he just leaves house with his bag of belongings, changes trains and ultimately reaches Kumbakonam back to his home in Salai Street. His house is being looked after by a caretaker and her daughter who are surprised to see him. The *Tamas Guna* of lack of self-control in the man protagonist is highlighted by Narayan when he writes of Viswanath's eating habits at seventy years of age.

> The house was filled all the time with smell of frying-chips, bondas, pakodas and sweets. Vishwa was a very contented man now.

He had a sturdy constitution which withstood all the gluttony he was indulging in (90).

The *Tamas Guna* of lack of self-control peaks in Viswa when he marries the caretaker's daughter in a quiet, simple ceremony. He is seventy-five and the girl is seventeen. He marries her to shock and spite his family, all of whom seem hostile to him. The caretaker and her daughter, in time, nag him to make them his family and eye his house, his precious stones and his money. To speed up their control on him and his property, the woman consults the local wiseacre, explaining the difficulties her son-in-law was creating. The wiseacre gives her a packet in which are two pills to be given to him with his food with a promise that Viswa would then follow his wife like a lamb and treat the mother as his guru. On the following Friday she prepares a special feast. Vishwa, a confirmed glutton, is so pleased that he eats all the delicacies followed by the almond and milk payasam in a silver bowl. Before serving it, the woman manages to dissolve the two pills in the silver bowl. The lack of self-control costs Vishwa his life and his end comes suddenly.

The above men protagonists are influenced by the dominating quality of **lack of Self-control**, a primary trait of *Tamas Guna.* This characteristic is evident in their personality and their inter-personal relationships throughout the course of the novel.

Delusion

Delusion is a belief or impression which is not real. It is one of the major characteristics of *Tamas Guna* as it makes a person dream, fantasise, hallucinate and live in self-deception. With delusion, arises sloth, which is being physically and emotionally inactive. It can also be either an outright refusal or merely a carelessness in the performance of one's duties. It leads to wasting due to lack of use, concerning a person, place, thing or skill.

In his novel, *The World of Nagaraj*, R.K. Narayan's man protagonist Nagaraj shows the predominance of *Tamas Guna.* His approach to life, to relationships and to work, is delusionary. He carries a belief which is not real. His dream is to write a thesis on sage *Narada,* but starting from the very first page of the novel to the last, he gives excuses for not getting any work done. Thus, he lives in self-deception. He weaves around himself a mirage, where he bluffs himself saying that when everything is in order, his work shall get started. Things never are to his satisfaction and so the work never gets started.

When asked why he wants to write his thesis on Narada, Nagaraj has an answer ready. Narayan writes:

> 'Why Narada?', thereby starting Nagaraj on the celestial sage who had a curse on his back that unless he spread a gossip a day his head would burst. The sage floated along with ease from one world to another among the fourteen worlds above and below this earth, carrying news and gossip, [often causing clashes between gods and demons, demons and demons and between creatures of the earth. Ultimately, of course, such clashes and destruction proved beneficial in a cosmic perspective. Evil destroyed itself. That was Nagaraj's thesis (3).

Nagaraj lives in the delusion of not working because he is not greedy for money. Rather he shirks responsibility and does no work. 'Thank God I don't have to think of money. I'm not greedy, that's why I'm happy', he says (4). He is lazy because after the division of property, he gets a thousand rupees from the bank deposits left by his father. Narayan portrays his personality dominated by *Tamas Guna* when he writes:

> ......while he had only been watching and wool-gathering, which were important activities in his scheme of living. Watching and brooding had a subtle value which people never realised. Left to himself he was prepared to sit on the pyol the whole day, looking on the life and movement of Kabir Street (7).

Nagaraj does not respond to situations and explains it with 'What would be the point in losing temper?' (8). Besides, he is so under the *Tamas Guna* of sloth that he believes 'too much of thinking is no good, rather fatiguing' (9). Even though he is a married man, he does not want to take responsibility of his wife. He finds an excuse to shirk work to write his thesis. For not being able to get his work started, he tries to put blame on other people or situations. He decides to wear ochre clothes because he lives in the delusion that wearing ochre clothes will help him concentrate on his work. He fools himself by believing the sanyasi who tells him:

> ....your mind should be only on God, not on money or the family. (Your) thoughts must be away from all sensual matters, free from *kama*, *krodha*, *lobha* and *moha*. You must observe silence, become deaf to other people's voices, never pay attention to it, even if there is an urgent telegram (11-2).

Highlighting the *Tamas Guna* of delusion in Nagaraj, Narayan writes:

> Now in his ochre robe he felt transformed. While he was in this dress, his wife was not to bring up any domestic matter or any letter in the post, never call him to the street door, even if an emperor knocked. She had to conduct herself as if he had ceased to exist. His mind worked further on the theme. It was a state of being dead for some moments each day. His guru, the Town Hall sanyasi, had explained, It's good to experience death a little each day so that when your time is up you will slip into the state effortlessly. You will realise how noble and welcome it is- then Death will not be dreaded and avoided. You will overcome death itself...(12).

Throughout the course of the novel, Nagaraj wiles away his time doing nothing constructive. Every morning it is the same routine for him. After eating breakfast, he would first stop at Kanni's stall at the market corner. Kanni was his schoolmate and now ran a shop which sold cigarettes, soda, beetle leaves and tobacco for chewing. After partaking of the beetle leaves, he would retreat to the Grove Street Sari Centre where 'attendants heaped on his table registers and ledgers and cash bills, which Nagaraj scrutinised and entered in the appropriate column in his books' (23). Nagaraj is so lazy that he does not wish to be punctual or regular in his work and so he works 'free for Coomar; no pay packet at the beginning of a month'. His logic is 'I don't need it and this arrangement leaves me free to come and go when I like'(24). Nagaraj does not want to work and so he is glad that his brother 'insisted upon being given all the land and coconut garden in the village along with the farmhouse and cattle' (33).

He is thankful that 'the fellow wants them' for he 'couldn't have stood the smell of cattle shed even for five minutes...' (33). The *Tamas Guna* impacts the man protagonist to such an extent that he spends evenings watching the activity of crows.

His brother comments on his attitude. Narayan writes:

> Gopu glared at him in anger, 'You are strange, impossible. You have no idea what to do, where and when. You exist from day to day like a cow chewing the cud and staring at space...'(41).

And further, 'Don't get up and try to escape, You have not lost that habit yet! Listen to me'(42) when Nagaraj does not react to his rude comments. Whenever there is an unpleasant situation, instead of resolving it, Nagaraj goes into a state of self-deception and all he thinks of is starting his thesis on Narada. Narayan writes about Nagaraj's delusionary state:

> 'Narada crated strife, no doubt, by passing disturbing gossip from one quarter to another, but it always proved beneficial in the long run, in an eternal perspective. Must write about him from this angle. Must write in English, of course, so that the book is widely read and people understand the concept of Narada. Must start writing on a good day lie Vijayadasami, the day of the Goddess of Learning. But I'm not a writer, must be helped by someone in the line. Must consult the Talkative Man, if I can stop him for a moment when he emerges from his home while starting on his rounds. Or Professor Lindham of Albert Mission School'....... Wait till I write my book' (44-45).

When Tim, son of Nagaraj's elder brother comes and stays with Nagaraj because he does not want to stay with his parents in the village, Gopu blames Nagaraj for it. He believes that 'Tim's prejudice against village life was due to Nagaraj's openly expressed aversion to the smell of cattle and cattleshed and his contempt for gobar gas' (51). However, Nagaraj offers no explanation to prove otherwise. Instead of talking to Tim or guiding him, Nagraj's main occupation becomes watching Tim's movements- on the sly. He pretends indifference and preoccupation but keeps an eye on Tim. He rises earlier than Tim, before seven in the morning. He pauses before Tim's door to detect the sound of movement inside. Nagaraj gets perturbed when one day he detects a faint alcohol flavour in the air. Nagaraj confronts Tim but Tim lies to him. Shirking responsibility of work and relationships is so much a part of Nagaraj's personality that this incident leaves him exhausted. Narayan writes:

> Worry had been a luxury unknown to Nagaraj till now. Nowadays when he sat on the pyol he realised that his mind had lost its poise. His thoughts constantly revolved round the subject of Tim, with many questions unanswered and he found it exhausting (61).

Nagaraj wants to confront Tim. However, *Tamas Guna* of delusion and inactivity makes him avoid all conversation. Thus, though his opening lines should have been, as soon as Tim appeared at the door, 'Tim, don't go away before I have a word with you,' in a firm, unambiguous tone' (67), Nagaraj just keeps quiet. He explains his behaviour thus:

> ......But one can't fling such a sentence at another just waking up- as bad as stabbing a sleeping king. One should allow a decent margin of the time for such things. (67).

So inactive is Nagaraj that when he finally agrees to talk to Tim about his suspicious activities, Sita says, 'I'm glad you are stirring yourself after all' (70). In fact, Nagaraj himself realises that he has 'achieved nothing' and that 'the problem of Tim remained where it began' (71). When the headmaster of Albert Mission School informs Nagaraj about Tim's absence from school he just sits 'brooding' (71). Instead of taking any action he wants to pick up his 'ochre dress' so that he can 'remain dumb' (80). Nagaraj's *Tamas Guna* of delusion is highlighted by Narayan as he writes:

> Nagaraj felt like banging his fist on the door to get Tim out. But all that he could do was to pace the hall up and down, sunk in thought. Sita left him with a significant glance at the door and retired to the bedroom. Nagaraj would have preferred to go out on to the pyol, peer into the silent dark street and clarify his thoughts, but Sita had bolted and barred the massive door........(81).

The man protagonist does not see anything simply because he does not want to, because he wants to take no responsibility of action. When Tim comes home drunk one day, Nagaraj does not correct him. He fools himself by saying, "I sniffed, but did not smell anything". To this

Sita's reply is, 'You don't smell anything because you don't want to'(82). Events take a turn and Tim gets married. His wife Saroja comes to stay in Nagaraj's house. As a part of her daily routine, she sings to the tune of Harmonium every morning. The delusionary Nagaraj finds yet another excuse for not working on his thesis on Narada. He blames his lack of concentration on the distraction made by the sound of harmonium and Saroja's singing. His list of explanation is endless. In his words:

> 'Narada! You are a god, I now understand. Forgive my doubts. Give me the power to write about you; when it comes out, men and women will worship you, But how am I to proceed? I must find a pundit who knows the subject' (94).

Excuses continue and Nagaraj blames his failure to write the thesis on ignorance of the *Sanskrit* language. He then takes the help of his friend 'The Talkative man' to find a pundit who will teach him the *Sanskrit* language- 'Deva Basha'(95). Only then can he start to write about Dev Narada. Finally, after much deliberation when 'The Talkative Man' is successful in arranging a meeting with the pundit, the *Tamas Guna* of delusion surfaces again and Nagaraj says, 'I am not the pundit's slave to be summoned or thrown out as he pleases' (104). When The Talkative Man insists on Nagaraj meeting the pundit, Nagaraj shirks the meeting by saying, 'Why is this fellow taking so much interest in me? I had better abandon my project' (104).

Although he strongly feels that the project on 'Narada cannot be abandoned and it is his 'whole life's aim' (113), he keeps postponing it. The lack of a notebook is another excuse he has and goes to buy one:

> ...... 'I want a very good notebook to write in -'
>
> 'Tell me whether bound or unbound, how many pages....' 'Nicely bound-'
>
> 'Nicely bound-? We have a good variety....' He turned to the boy, who was just limping in after his tea and cried, 'Hey, go up and fetch the wo-hundred-page Crow-brand'... He explained, 'I am beginning an important work on Narada...' (119).

Throughout the course of the novel, he keeps planning to write, but the project never really gets started. Nagaraj fools himself everyday by saying, '......from tomorrow I am going to be very, very busy' (121). He further deludes himself by believing that he will 'write a second book on Viswamitra and may be a whole series to be called 'Sages of India' (123). When he finally starts to write, he dilly-dallies with the choice of words:

> 'Once upon a time there was Narada...' Critics would sneer, 'Is this writer a thousand years old? Could almost be a contemporary of Narada......' He abandoned 'Once upon a time' and was biting the pen to think of a fresh start. He was not familiar with modern literature; his knowledge was confined to texts taught by Professor Kumar... (128).

Narayan writes:

> The literary struggle went on for a week. He constantly pored over his notes and wrote down in the belief that if you plunged in, the right passage would emerge. He suddenly said to himself, 'Do you think that the writers always thought over and then wrote? No sir, just inspiration. What is this thing called inspiration? Something that is churned out of a lot of mental struggle, something that has to be dug out and at the end it comes out like the spring at the bottom of a well.' This analogy somehow soothed his soul as a piece of discovery and a clue. 'Plunge straight in and you will come up with a pearl oyster.' So he decided to plunge into 'Once upon a time' and watch for developments. 'One can always erase the first sentence and put something else in its place to satisfy readers.' So he began briskly, 'Once upon a time all the gods in heaven were agitated......' He paused to ask himself, 'What were they agitated about?' He sat thinking for a while and added, '......about various things... about the state of the universe where Evil was rampant......' rampant? I have never used the expression in my life. Must look into a dictionary (128-9).

Nagaraj does not continue his writing because he cannot find the dictionary. He plans to get up early in the morning to continue with his writing. The next day he wears the ochre robe, 'picks up his notebooks' and utters a 'brief invocation to Saraswathi, the goodness of learning and enlightenment' (135) before embarking on his journey of writing the thesis. However, now he blames his brother and his nephew for burdening him with their problems and therefore his lack of concentration. Later though he fills up five books, the notes seem incomprehensible to him. There is no trace of the main character and none of the notes make sense to him.

> He felt desperate and cried out, 'Sita, come here!'...... Nagaraj pushed across the table a bundle of notebooks and said, 'if you need paper for lighting the oven, take these, take these away' (179).

John Theime writes:

> Nagaraj finds three local repositories of potential information on Narada and they represent three possible modes of writing available to the South Indian novelist. The first is a Sanskrit pundit, Kavu, who lectures Nagaraj on the need to be able to read the "Language of Gods" (WN 96) in order to have access to ancient Hindu wisdom... The third is the stationer Bari, who comes from a part of North India, Aligarh, where Narada is supposed to be particularly revered… (174).

Nagaraj is never able to come out of the *Tamas Guna* of delusion. He promises himself that 'Whatever may happen', he will start writing again from the next day 'at seven a.m.', 'even if the heavens fall' (181). Tim who had earlier left Nagaraj's house with his wife Saroja returns and so Nagaraj finds yet another reason not to write. He blames the noise of the harmonium as the distracting factor. Instead of questioning Tim about his activities while he was away and now his return, Nagaraj's reasoning for keeping quiet is:

> I am only a milestone. I stay and others come and pass. I must only watch, not ask questions. Tim's life and actions are, as ever, a mystery. But God has not endowed me with a temperament to solve mysteries. I have to accept them, that's all... I do not mind anything except that huge harmonium... (183-4).

Hence, the above man protagonist is heavily under the predominant trait of the *Tamas Guna* of **Delusion.**

Ignorance

Ignorance is a state of being uninformed (lack of knowledge). It also refers to a state of mind which is unenlightened, ill-informed, oblivious, unacquainted or unconscious. The word *ignorant* is an adjective describing a person in the state of being unaware and is often used as an insult to describe individuals who deliberately ignore or disregard important information or facts. Ignorance is distinguished from stupidity, although both can lead to 'unwise' acts. Ignorance can stifle learning, especially if the ignorant believe that they are not ignorant. A person who falsely believes s/he has knowledge will not seek clarification of beliefs thus doing more harm than good.

Writer Thomas Pynchon articulated about the scope and structure of one's ignorance:

> Ignorance is not just a blank space on a person's mental map. It has contours and coherence and for all I know rules of operation as well. So as a corollary to [the advice of] writing about what we know, maybe we should add getting familiar with our ignorance and the possibilities therein for writing a good story.

The legal principle that *ignorantia juris non excusat,* literally "ignorance of the law is no excuse", stands for the proposition that the law applies also to those who are unaware of it.

In his novel, *The Financial Expert*, R.K. Narayan highlights his man protagonist under the *Tamas Guna* of ignorance. Margayya is ignorant of his self, his purpose in life, his relationships and his work. It is the *Tamas Guna* of ignorance that impacts his personality in a way that he becomes cold to others' needs. Rather he becomes blinded by greed. He concentrates on earning more and more money. Whether it is by fair or unfair means, holds no importance to him. The man protagonist is in the business of lending money, on interest, to people. People call him Margayya. Narayan writes that the name is purely derivative: 'Marga' meant 'The Way' and 'Ayya' was an honorific suffix: taken together it denoted one who showed the way. He showed the way out to those in financial trouble (1). He is shown by Narayan to be unsympathetic to other people's troubles. When people can not pay up, Margayya tells them, "I am not concerned with all that- how you pay or what you do. You may perhaps pledge your life or your wife's sarees. It is none of my concern: all that I want to know is whether you are paying an instalment now or not" (4). Even though he is growing old, Margayya is reluctant to buy spectacles because it costs money. On his wife's insistence he does go to buy one from the proprietor of the shop who had been his playmate years ago, takes 'the glasses on trial' and forgets 'to go that way again'. On being reminded by the optician to pay up, he is snubbed by Margayya:

> Haven't you the elementary courtesy to know the time and place for such reminders? What greater insult can a man face than this sort of thing? What will an onlooker think? I am busy from morning to night - no time even for a cup of coffee in the afternoon! All right, it doesn't matter. Will you send someone to my house? I'm not able to use those glasses either. I wanted to come and exchange them if possible, but-...... How can you ask for our joint-signature? It's risky to do it even for one's own brother (5).

He does not understand the importance of his brother. He is 'known to be on throat-cutting terms' (21) with his brother's family. He is intimidated by status and money. He thinks that anyone with power and money has the right to threaten people. He states:

> He has every right because he has more money, authority, dress, looks- above all, more money. It's money which gives people all this. Money alone is important in this world. Everything else will come to us naturally if we have money in our purse (21).

He believes that when he has enough money, people will learn to behave with him.

He tells his wife:

> Even you will learn to behave with me when I have money. Your rudeness now is understandable. For isn't there a famous saying: 'He that hath not is spurned even by his wife; even the mother that bore him spurns him?' It was a very wise man who said it. Well, you will see. I'll not carry about that barber's box any more and I'll not be seen in this torn dhoti. I will become respectable like anyone else. That secretary will have to call me 'Mister' and stand up when I enter. No more torn mats and dirty, greasy sarees for you. Our boy will have a cycle, he will have a suit and go to a

> convent in a car. And those people" (he indicated the next house) "will have to wonder and burst their hearts with envy. He will have to come to me on his knees and wait for advice. I have finished with those villagers" (22).

Margayya can insult people for lack of money. This pleasure pricks his veins and thrills his body. Highlighting the man protagonist's *Tamas Guna* of ignorance leading to his greed for money and more money, Narayan writes:

> People did anything for money. Money was men's greatest need, like air or food. People went to horrifying lengths for its sake, like collecting rent on a dead body: yet this didn't strike Margayya in his present mood as so horrible as something to be marvelled at. It left him admiring the power and dynamism of money, its capacity to make people do strange deeds. He saw a toddy tapper going a hundred feet up a cocoanut tree and he reflected: "Morning to night he wears a loin cloth and goes up tree after tree for fifty years or more just for the eight annas he gets per tree." He saw offices and shops opened and people sweating and fatiguing themselves, all for money. Margayya concluded that they wanted money because they wanted fellows like the Secretary of the Co-operative Bank to bow to them, or to have a fellow like Arul Doss speak to them with courtesy, or so that they might wear unpatched dhoties and be treated seriously (28).

When Balu, his little son, throws away his accounts book in the gutter, he is perturbed, but reasons it saying, 'A man whom the Goddess of Wealth favours need not worry much. He can buy all the knowledge he requires. He can afford to buy all the gifts that Goddess Saraswathi holds in her palm' (51). So blinded is he by his greed for wealth that he attracts one Dr Pal in his life. Dr Pal shows him the manuscript of a book he wishes to publish. On turning the pages, a chapter-heading catches his eye: 'Philosophy and the Practice of Kissing' and 'Basic Principles of Embracing'. He turns over the pages and starts to read the first sentence of the opening chapter: "Man embraces woman and woman embraces man ……." (67).

He immediately feels interested. Briskly turning over the leaves, he comes upon the title sheet and reads it out aloud: 'Bed-Life or the

Science of Marital Happiness'. Dr Pal explains that the book was a branch of Sociology and that a thousand years ago Vatsyayana wrote his Kama-Sutra or 'Science of Love'. He insists that the 'subject must be understood by every man and woman. If people understood and practised this science there would be more happiness in the world' (68).

Margayya's greed for money makes him visit an astrologer. On his prediction that Margayya can earn pots and pots of money, he spends the next forty days offering prayers to Goddess Saraswati. Margayya visualises his future:

> How was wealth going to flow in? When he became rich, suppose he bought from his brother the next house too, tempting him with a handsome cash offer.......... He realised that this was his major concern in life. He would be a victorious man if he could bring his brother to his knees and make him part with his portion of the house; and then he would knock down the partition wall... (70).

He does not flinch from offering prayers to the Goddess because all he needs is money. Narayan writes:

> ... Each day it took him eight hours of repetition to complete the thousand and then he reverently put the black paste on his forehead, lit the camphor, called in his wife and child and sprinkled the holy water on them. His jaws ached, his tongue had become dry...... he felt faint with hunger, since he had to fast completely while praying. He followed this course for forty days. When he emerged from the little room, he had a beard and moustache and hair on his nape......Margayya had lost ten pounds in weight: much of the padding on his waist and jowl had gone (70-1).

The story unfolds and Margayya becomes very rich by getting the manuscript of Dr Pal published as a book named *Domestic Harmony*. The book gets Margayya huge business and he tells his wife, 'We can live differently hereafter, I think. A lot of money is coming in' (102). The wisdom that time passes quickly and money is but a temporary possession, is not prevalent in the man protagonist. Rather the *Tamas Guna* of ignorance impacts his disposition. He shows off his wealth by admitting the six-year-old Balu to the *Town Elementary School*. He makes a great performance of it. He takes his son in a decorated motor with pipes and drums through the Market Road: the traffic is held up for half an hour. Margayya makes Balu sit with the 'top of his head shaved, with diamonds sparkling on his ear lobes and a rose garland round his neck, in a taxi with four of his picked friends by his side'(105). Just because Margayya has money, he becomes the school secretary due to which Balu enjoys special privilege with the teachers. [P]eople would look at him and say, "Well, there goes Margayya's son. Lucky fellows, these sons of businessmen" (111).

The *Tamas Guna* of ignorance makes Margayya indulge in false talks. Though it is by the sale of the book *Domestic Harmony* that Margayya makes money, he gets only 'a single copy' (118) of it into his house. He does not want Balu 'to know that there is such a book' (118). Highlighting ignorance in Margayya, Narayan writes:

> His wife expressed deep appreciation of this precaution. Margayya felt further impelled to add, "I don't want people to say that Balu enjoys all the money earned through *Domestic Harmony.* I would do anything to avoid it." He felt very heroic when he said that. He seemed to swell with his goodness, nobility and importance and the clean plans he was able to make for his son (118).

Margayya becomes unscrupulous when it comes to earning money. Though initially he enters into a partnership deal with Lal, the publisher, Margayya now abandons his interest in *Domestic Harmony* for a lump- sum money. He then sets up a business with Dr Pal as his tout. However, he fools people and himself by saying:

> ... He felt that he must do something to enlighten their minds. He would not be a banker to them, but a helper, a sort of money doctor who would help people to use their money properly with the respect due to it. He would educate society anew in all these matters (123).

Narayan makes the man protagonist in *The Financial Expert* preoccupied with money.

Margayya believes:

> ...... money is the greatest factor in life and the most ill-used. People don't know how to tend it, how to manure it, how to water it, how to make it grow and when to pluck its flowers and when to

> pluck its fruits. What most people now do is to try and eat the plant itself...." (132).

The *Tamas Guna* of ignorance manifests in Margayya as extreme greed for money. Narayan writes:

> He was a specialist in money and his mind always ran on lines of scientific inquiry whenever money came in question. He differentiated with great subtlety between money, riches, wealth and fortune. It was most important people should not mistake one for the other (134).

Margayya is shown to be a miser and *Tamas Guna* of ignorance that life and its riches are permanent, makes him behave selfishly. So much so that he refuses to lend such a petty thing as an umbrella to people. If he saw anyone going out in the rain in imminent danger of catching and perishing of pneumonia, he would rather let him face his fate, than offer him the protection of his umbrella. He felt furious when people thought that they could ask for an umbrella. "They will be asking for my skin next," he often commented when his wife found fault with his attitude. Another argument he advanced was, "Do people ask for each other's wives? Don't they manage to have one for themselves?' (144). Narayan portrays Margayya as a person whose life depends on earning money and more money. Though his business is to lend money on interest, or mortgage property etc., he does it in ways which can give him maximum profit even though it may require succumbing to falsehood. Narayan states:

Margayya was the one man who lent easily. He made the least fuss about the formalities, but he charged interest in so many subtle ways and compounded so deftly that the moment a man signed his bonds, he was more or less finished. He could never hope to regain his possessions-especially if he allowed a year or two to elapse.

There were debt relief laws and such things. But Margayya nullified their provisions because the men for whom the laws were made were enthusiastic collaborators in his scheme, and everything he did looked correct on paper. He acquired a lot of assets. But he lost no time in selling them and realising their cash again and stored it in an iron safe at home. "What am I do to with property?" he said, "I want only money, not brick and lime or mud," he reflected when he reconverted his attached property into cash (182-3).

The story takes a complicated turn when Balu, now a young man runs away from home. A few weeks later, Margayya receives a letter from Madras saying that Balu is dead. Margayya rushes to Madras, finds out that Balu is not really dead and brings him back. He then wants to get him married. Margayya decides to get his son married to the daughter of a man who owns tea estates in Mempi Hills. To achieve this goal for selfish reasons of getting more money, he consults the astrologer with their horoscopes 'purely as a formality'(185). When the astrologer denies their match, Margayya pushes him out of his house. Dr Pal tells Margayya to find a different astrologer who re-arranges the stars of 'Balu to suit the circumstances'(187). The two get married and start to stay at an establishment at Lawley Road. Even though the house becomes lonely and Margayya's wife misses her son and daughter-in-law, Margayya notices no difference. His mind is busy 'formulating a new plan' which would 'rocket him to undreamt heights of financial success' (192). Times passes and Margayya becomes a grandfather.

Although the protagonist is rich, he is a big miser. When he receives applications for charity, he gets angry and says:

> What do they take me for? A Magic Pot?... I do not work hard and wear myself out in order to give gifts. Who came to my help in those days when I was in difficulties?

Day after day, he becomes more obsessed with money. Narayan writes:

> The moment he reached home, he counted the notes again, bundled them in tidy little batches, the lovely five rupee and ten rupee and that most handsome piece of paper the green hundred rupee note. He counted his cash over and over again and locked it up in his safe and shut the door. It would be nearly midnight when he finished the counting and rose to have his dinner (199).

With work ahead, he has no patience for food. He goes to his office almost as soon as he gets up from bed and returns home at indefinite hours. Things go on as Margayya would have liked them to be. However, with Dr Pal as his constant companion, Balu starts to play cards, chew tobacco and betel leaves, sometimes drink and also womanise. To continue the leisure, Balu needs money and now he asks Margayya for his share of property. The *Tamas Guna* of ignorance and greed sees Margayya as a lonely, disturbed man. He goes to his son's house where he gets to know of his son's bad company from his daughter-in-law. He is very upset, gets impatient and enters into a brawl with Dr Pal. To avenge his insult, Dr Pal tells all the people in the city false stories about Margayya going bankrupt. The result is thus:

> One after another they came with their receipts. Margayya returned their cash without a murmur. The street became congested with people converging on his house; people hung about his steps and windows. He bolted the front door and dealt with them through the window (215).

It may have taken Margayya a long time to earn all the money, but he loses all of it in no time. When people come to ask for their money, Margayya has no choice but to return it. By the same evening about four o' clock all the cash in the house is gone. The mail sacks lie about empty and slack. Still there are 'seas and seas of human heads stretching to the horizon, human faces at their most terrifying' (215). Margayya gets so terrified that he calls his brother next-door for help. Margayya files for insolvency even though it means putting his reputation at stake. The *Tamas Guna* of ignorance leading to greed leaves Margayya a lonely, poor man. His son along with his wife and child have to return to Margayya's house as he can no longer support them with money. Narayan ends the novel with Margayya planning to return to his old practice of lending money sitting under the banyan tree. The closing line where Margayya refers to his grand child, 'Now get the youngster here. I will play with him. Life has been too dull without him in this house' (218) shows some realisation of the importance of relationships over money. The entire novel, however, focuses primarily on the *Tamas Guna* of ignorance of the man protagonist Margayya. William Walsh writes:

> R.K. Narayan, as a conscious social writer, recognises the importance of money in the life of man, does not ignore the place of money in life nor does he moralise that money is the root cause

> of all evil. He gives money its due place in the life of the individual and in that of the community. He maintains that money is a very important thing in life as it satisfies our aims, aspirations and dreams. But notwithstanding the basic importance of money, the novelist thinks and believes that money is a good thing so long as it is only a means and is intended to serve a purpose. Its role is good up to a point, but it causes problems of different kinds when it becomes the summum bonum of man's life. When it becomes an end in itself it causes complications and leads up to undesirable and unfortunate results (95).
>
> Thus, the protagonist, Margayya, is dominated by the *Tamas Guna* of **Ignorance** and his entire personality is governed by this trait.

The men protagonists **Ramani** in *The Dark Room,* **Margayya** in *The Financial Expert,* **Nagaraj** in *The World of Nagaraj* and **Viswanath** in *Grandmother's Tale* show the predominance of *Tamas Guna.* Their characters as portrayed by Narayan are embedded in ignorance and delusion. They give in to their carnal desires and have no respect for relationships. The motive of their actions is greed. They are ignorant that life is a temporary journey and all respective actions have subsequent results. They disregard other people's emotions and focus on their selfish needs. It is the brilliance of R.K. Narayan that he is able to highlight the *Tamas Guna* in the above-mentioned men protagonists.

5

Comparison of Narayan's Men Protagonists with the Select Ones of Mulk Raj Anand and Raja Rao

Dr Mulk Raj Anand and Raja Rao are contemporaries of R.K. Narayan. The trio is best known as the founding writers of Indian English fiction. Raja Rao (1908 – 2006) was an Indian writer of English language novels and short stories, whose works are deeply rooted in Hinduism. *The Serpent and the Rope* (1960), a semi-autobiographical novel narrating a search for spiritual truth in Europe and India, established him as one of the finest Indian prose stylists and won him the Sahitya Akademi Award in 1964.

Raja Rao was born in a South Indian Brahmin family in 1909 in Mysore. After passing grade tenth from Hyderabad, he went to Aligarh for higher education. He took his B.A. degree from Nizam College, Hyderabad. He was awarded government scholarship by the Hyderabad University to go to France to continue his study of French literature. He lived in France from 1928 to 1939, returned to India on the outbreak of World War II in 1940 and again went to France in 1946. He lived there till 1956. It was in France, that his first novel *Kanthapura* (1938) was written. His second novel *The Serpent and the Rope* (1960), published after a gap of twenty-two years, has France and India as its background thus revealing to the reader that Raja Rao had also fully absorbed and assimilated the culture of the West.

Through this novel Raja Rao founded a new genre of the novel - the philosophical novel. This novel is also regarded as the spiritual autobiography of the novelist. The time of the story is around the year 1950 and action constantly shuttlecocks between India, France and England. The story is narrated by the man protagonist Ramaswamy or Rama. He is a young and educated man belonging to a rich zamindar family in South India. He goes to France for research studies. There he meets Madeleine, a young French Lady, a teacher at one of the university colleges and falls in love her. They get married and live happily together in Axis near Paris. A son is born to them, but unfortunately, he dies soon after. This is a great shock to Madeleine and she cannot be her usual self again. The story proceeds and new characters are introduced by Rao in the narrative. When Rama is in Europe, his father dies and he has to hurry back home to India. He takes Little Mother (The third wife of his father) and his baby brother, Sridhara, to Benaras for the last rites of his father. A detailed account is given of the city of Benaras and its philosophical significance. From Benaras they go to Allahabad where he meets Pratap Singh who is betrothed to Savithri, the young Western educated daughter of the Raja of Surajpur. She does not want to marry him. She is back home from Cambridge at the time and Rama is introduced to her. Rama is fascinated by her and the meeting is far-reaching in its consequences. From Allahabad they go to Haridwar and then return to their home. Having settled affairs at home, Rama returns to France to complete his work on the thesis. The novel proceeds and the circumstances see an emotion-driven Rama accepting Savithri as his wife. However, since he is already in a marriage with Medeleine he advises Savithri to go back to India and marry the husband destined for her. Savithri eventually marries Pratap Singh.

Rama constantly receives letters from ‘mother’ and his two sisters. He comes back to India when the marriage of his sister is settled, even though Medeleine is in the family way. He is expected to return to her in time for the delivery, but is prevented from doing so by his illness. His lungs are weak and now he throws out blood copiously to become seriously ill. Meanwhile, Madeleine has to undergo a Caesarian section and even though her life is saved, their second child dies. The shock received by Madeleine changes the whole course of their future life. On his return to France, Rama finds a great change in Madeleine.

She becomes a devout Buddhist, keeps fasts frequently and passes most of her time in prayer and meditation. She even goes on a long forty-one days fast and comes out of the ordeal successfully, Normal life with her is no longer possible and it is obvious that they must separate. However, they continue to live together for some time. Events take a turn, Medeleine become a *Sanyasni,* divorce proceedings are initiated and soon they are duly divorced. Rama continues to live in France, but without a home. Catherine and Georges, who live in Paris, befriend him and try to make him comfortable. He visits them frequently and is soon deeply attached to Vera, their only child. Ambiguity marks the end of the novel, for it is not clear whether Rama actually returns to India, or his attachment to Vera keeps him back in Paris.

Comparing the novels of R.K. Narayan with Raja Rao's, *The Serpent and the Rope,* with Modes of Nature as the focus, it can be said that though the influence of the three *Gunas* viz *Sattva, Rajas* and *Tamas* can be traced in the man protagonist, Ramaswamy, the predominance of one *Guna* over the other two is not stark. The influence of *Sattva Guna* of wisdom is reflected in Ramaswamy. He hails from a rich, Brahmin family of Mysore. A Brahmin is one who is 'devoted to truth' and 'who knows Brahma'. Rama is certainly a Brahmin, for he can read and recite the *Upanishads* at the age of four and also knows the *Brahma Sutras*. He has a penetrating intellect and is always keen to study, analyse and discuss in order to know the truth. Well-versed in Hindu Philosophy and Metaphysics, he is eager to know the truth about other religions and philosophies. His mission in life is to see the West hold India in high esteem. He takes to the study of History, as against his father wish for him to study Mathematics. He calls himself a 'holy vagabond' and the epithet is justified. He travels across many countries and meets a number of people. He is always keen to have a philosophical discussion with them- particularly on Vedantic philosophy- so that he may bring about a better understanding of India in the West. Philosophical and metaphysical truths constantly come out of his lips in the form of aphorisms. Though he is a Brahmin by virtue of his learning and his life-long quest for truth, he has no love for rituals and ceremonies. Broad-minded and liberal in his outlook, he is entirely free from the orthodoxy and superstitions which obscure and disfigure the essential nobility and greatness of Hindu religion.

The *Rajas Guna* of passion impacts Rama's personality when he meets Madeleine. He gets attracted to her by their common interest in History. The physical attributes of Madeleine leave him spellbound and arouse in Ramaswamy, the *Rajas Guna* of passion. Rao writes:

> Her hair was gold and her skin for an Indian was like the unearthed marble with which we built our winter palaces. Cool, with the lake about one and the peacock strutting in the garden below (10-11).

The *Rajas Guna* of restless activity in Rama can be traced by studying his childhood years. His mother dies when he is only seven years old. His father remarries a second time and then a third time. Rama suffers from a sense of spiritual loneliness all his life. Though he is treated with love and affection by those he comes in contact with, in none of his relationships does he find satisfaction and sense of oneness which his soul yearns for. This inner loneliness, the yearning for a perfect unison of mind and spirit, makes him turn from one woman to another, ever dissatisfied, ever hankering for a perfection which always eludes his grasp. His physical weakness can also be the outcome of his psychological stress. When his marriage with Madeleine is wrecked, he feels that he has lost his moorings in Europe. He has also lost them in India, for Little Mother goes away to live with her married daughter. He feels lonely, without a home and confused. It is only a guru who can show him a way out of his troubles and he hopes to find such a Guru in Travancore.

In addition, *Tamas Guna* of delusion gets highlighted in Rama's personality. In his words:

> I am a tired man. I am of a tired race which for three (four of five) thousand years has led such a studious, thin-fed, sedentary existence, that our nose and throat, our ears, tongues and eyes, have lost somewhat in native agility (145).

He shuns taking responsibility of his relationships, of his actions and wants to tear his 'clothes and set off to the Himalayas'. He wishes to free himself from the shackles of Brahminism. He is not happy. His sadness is intellectual and psychological. From his sadness, he seeks, 'refuge in history and metaphysics' (44).

The spectacle of life terrifies him and he wishes to be a yogi. Like the men protagonists of R.K. Narayan, Ramaswamy is in different roles – of a son, brother, husband, student, friend. However, unlike Narayan, the predominance of one particular *Guna* in Rao's man protagonist Ramaswamy can not be seen. Further, though the novel is hailed as a brilliant work of Raja Rao, the critics review it as a work heavily over-loaded with discussions of subtle metaphysical problems which are often beyond the comprehension of the average reader.

Mulk Raj Anand (1905 – 2004) was an Indian writer in English, notable for his depiction of the lives of the poorer castes in traditional Indian society. One of the pioneers of Indo-Anglian fiction, he was among the first Indian writers in English to gain an international readership. Anand is admired for his novels and short stories, which have acquired the status of being classic works of modern Indian English literature. His writings are noted for their insight into the lives of the oppressed and their analyses of impoverishment, exploitation and misfortune.

A writer's views and attitudes condition his work. They are resultant of a number of influences that operate upon him since childhood. Mulk Raj Anand is no exception. His heredity, social milleu, education, the books he read and the people he met, have all impacted the novelist. Mulk Raj Anand is a great humanist. He writes for the dignity of men irrespective of caste, creed and wealth. He attaches profound importance to art and poetry as instruments for developing whole men. His crusade against superstition, feudalism and imperialism are some of the chief characteristics of humanism. Anand was greatly influenced by Indian struggle for independence. He hated imperialism and was also disgusted by the hypocrisy of Indian feudal life. He was aware that many people suffered from poverty and squalor. It became Anand's aim as a novelist to focus attention on this suffering and thus to write what may fittingly be called 'epics of misery'. Karl Marx's writings influenced Anand. Anand writes:

> A whole new world was opened to me. All the threads of my past reading, which had got tied up in knots, seemed suddenly to straighten out and I began to see not only the history of India but the whole history of human society in some sort of inter-connection (22).

Untouchable (1935) is Anand's first novel. It brought him immense eminence and prestige. It narrates a day in the life of the man protagonist, Bakha, a sweeper. Unlike traditional sweepers, he struggles hard to lead a better life. He goes to clean the three rows of public latrines situated in the outcastes' colony. He has a sister named Sohini. Pandit Kalinath, the in-charge of the temple asks Sohini to come and sweep the courtyard of his house in the temple. He wants to molest her, but she protests. Bakha goes to the city to clean the streets on behalf of his father. There he touches an upper caste Hindu. The incident provikes abuses and humiliation. The novel ends with three solutions to the problem of untouchability: Christ, Gandhi and the Flush-system. Gandhi appears in person to speak on the evil of untouchability.

To quote E.M. Forster:

> The book has form, the action occupies one day and takes place in a small area. The great catastrophe of the touching takes place in the morning and poisons all that happens subsequently, even such pleasant episodes as the hockey match and the country walk. After a jagged course of ups and downs, we come to the solution, or rather to the three solutions, with which the book closes....... (Preface to *Untouchable*).

Untouchable is a sociological novel. It talks of injustice and exploitation to which one large section of the Hindu society is subjected to by others enjoying a higher status in the social hierarchy. The novel is about the life of the untouchables who have been victims of social injustice, oppression and exploitation. It deals not merely with the life and suffering of one individual untouchable, Bakha, but through Bakha it presents a gigantic problem of the Hindu society. Thus, the character of Bakha synonymous with all people who get exploited. The omission of article 'the' in the title before the word 'Untouchable' is another proof that the novel is not concerned with any particular individual but with the whole class of untouchables, of which the particular individual is but a representative. One day of Bakha's life mean's all the days in the lives of all Bakhas, the sweepers.

Comparing Bakha, the man protagonist of Mulk Raj Anand with the men protagonists of R.K. Narayan, one finds that the predominance of one particular *Guna* in the disposition of Bakha can not be traced.

The structure of the novel is such that it deals with showing the plight of the 'untouchable' community. It is heart-wrenching to read the apt and vivid description of the outcastes' colony. Anand writes and tells the readers how the colony is situated at a distance from the city. The surroundings of this colony are very dirty. The filth of latrines, the skins of the carcasses left to dry in its vicinity, the dung of donkeys, sheep, horses, cows and buffaloes go on sending foul smell. The atmosphere of the houses is suffocating. The absence of drainage system has made the quarter a marsh which gives out the most offensive smell. Bakha lives with his father and other members of the family in a one-roomed cottage, dark and dingy and entirely unfit for human habitation. It is in this single dirty room that they all sleep, cook and do store everything- their baskets, brooms and other tools of their occupation.

Tamas Guna is highlighted in a person due to the filthy surroundings. This aspect of the *Tamas Guna* comes to the fore when Anand writes how the effect of the dirty surroundings influence the souls of the outcastes. All the outcastes in the novel except Bakha have a corrupting and polluting influence of their surroundings on them. Rakha is a true representative of the caste he belongs to. Anand gives a pen-portrait of Rakha in all his filth:

> His tattered flannel shirt, grimy with the blowing of his ever-running nose, obstructed his walk slightly. The discomfort resulting from this, the fatigue, assumed or genuine, due to the work he had put in that morning, ... gave a rather drawn, long-jawed look to his dirty face on which the flies congregated in abundance to taste- of the sweet delights of the saliva on the corners of his lips (75).

By exposing untouchability, Anand offers a solution to it. He hints at three possible solutions: Gandhism, Conversion to Christianity and the flush-system leading to the economic and social upgradation of the untouchables. The last solution is acceptable to the hero of the novel more than any other.

Comparing Narayan's men protagonists with Anand's 'Bakha' and Rao's 'Ramaswamy', it can be ascertained that the predominance of one *Guna* over the other two is not very clear in the latter. The three *Gunas* are present albeit overlapping each other. The dynamics and the influence of one predominating *Guna* through the entire course of the novel is not stark in either Anand's *Untouchable* or Rao's *Serpant and the Rope.* It is the sheer genius of R.K. Narayan who, even though writes of ordinary men in ordinary situations, can create a storyline which can trace each protagonist under one predominating *Guna* through the entire course of the respective novel.

Conclusion

This study has combined

(1) R.K. Narayan's men protagonist in all his fifteen novels

(2) The Bhagvad Gita's Moksha's philosophy of three *Gunas* - *Sattva* (wisdom), *Rajas* (action) and *Tamas* (delusion).

R.K. Narayan, in his novels, portrays men protagonists in such a way that the predominance of one *Guna* over the other two, for example, *Sattva* atop *Rajas*/*Tamas*, *Tamas* aloft *Rajas/Sattva* or *Rajas* dominating over *Sattva/Tamas*, becomes evident in their personalities. These three modes of nature and their expressions through the men protagonists in Narayan's novels are not 'pure' categories or closed in separate boxes. However, the master craftsman gives an ample scope to study each man protagonist under the influence of one dominating *Guna* within specific contexts and circumstances.

The journey of researching Narayan's men protagonists under one highlighting *Guna* enables the understanding of *self.* His stories have subtle messages which inspire the readers to think, to find answers to complex conundrums of Who, When, Where, What and Why. Narayan in his writings and more importantly through the dialogues he gives his characters assists the journey of self-discovery.

Narayan adheres to the ancient Indian tradition where his writings reflect the deep belief in the theory of transmigration of soul, *karma* (action one performs), renunciation and reincarnation. N. Ram observes that Narayan's fiction is 'distinctive for its voice, its fusion of the comic with the sad and its philosophical depth. Studying the narrative technique of Narayan, Nityananda Pattanayak says that each of Narayan's novels have a message. To transmit that message, the author selects his devices carefully so as not to cause any imbalance between the matter and the manner of telling it. Narayan has a comic vision of life; his message is mostly covert; even themes of deep philosophical understandings are treated in a comic mode (271). William Walsh tries to delve into the psyche of Narayan's characters and considers that their entire lifestyle has been imperceptibly controlled by the Indian ethos and that, 'even the seedy, the stupid and vain, retain a peculiar, nuclear innocence'.

Sattva Guna denotes the influence of wisdom in thoughts, words and actions. Kindness, compassion and altruism are closely associated with wisdom. Without compassion, rationality and reason fail to prevail. These distinguishing features of the *Sattva Guna* are intermingled.

The men protagonists which show the influence of the predominating *Sattva Guna* are **Sriram** in Waiting *for the Mahatma* (1955), **Nataraj** in *The Man-Eater of Malgudi (*1961), **Jagan** in *The Vendor of Sweets* (1967), **Raman** in *The Painter of Signs* (1976*)* and **The Master** in *A Tiger for Malgudi* (1983). These men show qualities of altruism, empathy, wisdom, kindness, divinity and purity. Their actions lean strongly towards Gandhi's doctrine of love and non-violence. Characteristics, specific to *Sattva Guna*, which were studied in the above men protagonists are-

(a) Wisdom and Knowledge

(b) Compassion

(c) Following the Gandhian way of life

(d) Religious bent of Mind and Spirituality

The protagonist, Raman in the novel, *The Painter of Signs,* is shown to have traits bearing the *Sattva Guna* of **Wisdom and Knowledge** at the very beginning of the story. He is 'determined to establish the 'Age of Reason'. Narayan writes:

> "I want a rational explanation for everything", he cries, "otherwise my mind refuses to accept any statement..........I am a rationalist and I don't do anything unless I see some logic in it" (5).

The Man-Eater of Malgudi showcases the *Sattva Guna* of **Wisdom and Knowledge** in the protagonist, Nataraj's disposition. Comparison of Nataraj with Vasu, each symbolic of *Sattva Guna* and *Tamas Guna* respectively, brings out the importance of wisdom. The dialogues between the two characters are beautifully drawn. Vasu says, "I never forget", to which Nataraj replies, "and I never remember" (19). Deep philosophical message is depicted thus. To never remember a hurt, not hold a grievance, forget an insult and forgive unconditionally are essential qualities of the *Sattva Guna.*

In his novel, *The Vendor of Sweets*, Narayan brings out the *Sattva Guna* of **Compassion** in the protagonist Jagan's personality. Jagan notices simple things, which might be causing discomfort to others. He arranges for a chair for 'one Mr Noble, an Englishman, the District Collector, who came for lessons in astrology and found it painful to sit on the floor and found it even more painful to extricate himself from the sitting posture at the end of the lessons' (11). He is concerned for "that little girl in the yellow skirt, ask her what she wants. She has been standing there so long!" (12). *Sattva Guna* shines in his compassionate personality when he says, "If everyone gave up dining leaves, those engaged in the leaf trade would be thrown out of their profession and an alternative engagement would have to be found for them" (16). He is in the business of making and selling sweets. Yet he is opposed to the idea of making profits by unfair means. He does 'not like the idea of cheating' (80) his customers and believes that 'it is purity that is important' (90).

The *Sattva Guna* of **Following the Gandhian Way of Life** impacts Sriram after he comes in close association with Mahatma Gandhi in *Waiting for the Mahatma*. Gandhi ji's words to him, "You must look after your granny too, she must have devoted herself to bringing you up" (70) kindle a spark of empathy in Sriram. Further, Mahatma's speech: "before you aspire to drive the British from this country, you must drive every vestige of violence from your system. Remember that it is not going to be a fight with sticks and knives or guns but only with love" (77), inspire Sriram in his onward journey towards compassion and value of truth and non-violence.

In *A Tiger for Malgudi,* the *Sattva Guna* of **Religious bent of Mind and Spirituality** shines when Narayan makes The Master describe God as 'The creator, the great spirit pervading every creature, every rock and tree and the stars, a source of power and strength' (157-8). The Master sees the tiger as a life form having 'only the appearance of a tiger, but he is not one-inside he is no different from you and me' (146).

Sattva Guna of **Religious bent of Mind and Spirituality** is conveyed by Narayan in *The Man-Eater of Malgudi.* It is an allegory which shows that evil is self-destructive. The master storyteller writes:

> ...every demon appears in the world with a special boon of indestructibility. Yet the universe has survived all the rakshasas that were ever born. Every demon carries within him, unknown to himself, a tiny seed of self-destruction and goes up in thin air at the most unexpected moment. Otherwise, what will happen to humanity? (240).

G.S. Amur tries to perceive Narayan from the Indian perspective. He points out that since Narayan is deeply rooted in his own Hindu culture, his characters have all along been controlled by the values and ideals originating in his own culture. In 'India: a wounded civilisation', V.S. Naipaul reports a remark that Narayan made to him during a conversation in London in 1961: 'India will go on'. For Naipaul, this comment crystallizes what he views as Narayan's conservative belief in an old equilibrium, a stable social order, understood through a philosophy with roots in orthodox Hinduism.

The novels for research and the respective men protagonists under the impact of *Rajas Guna* are **Swaminathan** in *Swami and Friends* (1935), **Chandran** in *The Bachelor of Arts* (1937), **Krishna** in *The English Teacher* (1945), **Sampath** in *Mr. Sampath* (1949), **Raju** in *The Guide* (1956) and **Madhu** in *A Talkative Man* (1986). These men show qualities of action, restlessness, ambition, desire, obedience and passion. They have an ambition to succeed. They often get restless. Passionate about relationships, they wish to please their elders. They believe in doing their duty in sync with the pleasures of the flesh. Thus, predominance of *Rajas Guna* is reflected in their personalities. The following four characteristics prevalent under this *Guna* were undertaken for the study:

(a) Desire, Passion and Lust

(b) Attachment

(c) Obedience

(d) Ambition and Action

In the novel, *The Bachelor of Arts*, the protagonist, Chandran is totally under the *Rajas Guna* of **Desire, Passion and Lust.** Narayan showcases this when he writes:

> That night he (Chandran) went home very preoccupied. It was at five o'clock that he had met her and at nine he was still thinking of her. After dinner he did not squat on the carpet in the hall but preferred to go his room and remain alone there. He tried to read a little; he was in the middle of Well's Tono Bungay. He had found the book gripping, but now he felt it was obtrusive. He was irritated. He put away the book and sat staring at the wall. He presently realised that darkness would be more soothing. He blew out the lamp and sat in his chair (56-7).

In Narayan's novel, the man protagonist, Mr. Sampath is influenced by the *Rajas Guna* of **Desire, Passion and Lust**. His thought process under the *Rajas Guna* comes to the foray when he says:

> Some people say that every sane man needs two wives— a perfect one for the house and a perfect one outside for social life....I have the one. Why not the other? I have confidence that I will keep both of them happy and if necessary in separate houses. Is a man's heart so narrow that it cannot accommodate more than one? I have married according to Vedic rites: let me have one according to the civil marriage law... (179).

The protagoniost, Krishna, in *The English Teacher* is impacted and dominated by the *Rajas Guna* of **Attachment** throughout the novel. Krishna is in love with his wife and for Susila's comfort, he decides to buy a house. In sync with his motive, he takes her along to see a house. However, as circumstances would have it, Susila has to use a lavatory which is infested with flies and unfortunately, she gets down with typhoid. Though Krishna tries his best to save her, Susila dies. When Krishna takes her for cremation, the *Rajas Guna* of extreme attachment to his wife leaves him devastated. Narayan writes:

> ...they build up a pyre, place her on it, cover her up with layers of fuel...Leaving only face and the part of her chest out, four layers

> deep down. I pour ghee on and drop the fire......There are no more surprises and shocks in life, so that I watch the flame without agitation. For me the greatest reality is this and nothing else.... nothing else will worry or interest me in life hereafter (96).

Similarly, Narayan projects the *Rajas Guna* of **Obedience** in the novel, *Swami and Friends*. Swaminathan, the protagonist is under the impact of this highlighting *Guna*. Obedience without logic, brings fear of authority. One fails to 'reason' accurately. For example, when Swaminathan gives a list of things to be bought for his forthcoming exam and tells his father that the examinations begin the day after, the father shouts, "And yet you are wandering about the house like an unleashed donkey! What preposterous list is this? Do you think rupees, annas and paise drop from the sky?" (67). So terrified is Swaminathan of his father that he does not give any reason for his action. *Rajas Guna* of obedience gets highlighted in the personality of Chandran in all relationships with his elders. When Swaminathan fails to go to school, the headmaster canes him and says, "I will kill you if you keep on staring without answering my question" (124).

The *Rajas Guna* of **Ambition and Action** drives Raju's journey in Narayan's *The Guide*. The question of 'rich' verses 'successful' gets answered through Raju's personality which is heavily affected by the *Rajas Guna*. Narayan makes Raju question Nalini, 'Well you have a big household, a big car and what not-is that not enjoyment of life?' (194).

The Talkative Man, highlights the *Rajas Guna* of **Action** (non-stop talking is a primary mode of action) from the very first page when The Talkative Man says:

> They call me Talkative Man. Some affectionately shorten it to TM: I have earned this title, I suppose, because I cannot contain myself. My impulse to share an experience with others is irresistible, even if they sneer at my back. I don't care. I'd choke if I did not talk.... (1).

C.D. Narasimhaish regards Narayan as the product of Hindu middle - class ideologies. He points out that Narayan has an eye for the comic in life around him and that he telescopes the oddity in ordinary men 'within the accepted religious and social framework'.

In a whimsical 'Self-Obituary' Narayan imagines himself being charged (among other offences) with leaving his 'characters in mid-air, their destinies unsolved'. Swami (of *Swami and Friends*) standing on a railway platform watching a departing train, Chandran (of *The Bachelor of Arts*) cycling down the road and Savitri (of *The Dark Room*) sitting at a window. This is exactly what prompts the reader to find answers to complex questions. The reader can identify with the situations and the master craftsman opens the window to the reader's soul where the reader can reach the conclusion according to his own thought processes.

Researching Narayan's men protagonists under the influence of *Tamas Guna* makes the understanding of 'delusion' and 'ignorance' clear in reader's own disposition. Shirking work and making excuses for it becomes evident when analysing the men protagonists under *Tamas Guna*. The following characters of **Ramani** in *The Dark Room (*1938), **Margayya** in *The Financial Expert* (1952*)*, **Nagaraj** in *The World of Nagraj* (1990) and **Viswanath** in *Grandmother's Tale* (1992*)* are shown by Narayan to have qualities such as

(a) Lack of Self-control

(b) Delusion

(c) Ignorance

The protagonist, Ramani, in *The Dark Room* disrespects one of the most important relationships of the Hindu custom - that of his wife. The *Tamas Guna* of **Lack of Self-control** makes him have an affair outside of his marriage. He hurts his wife and lies to her. Throughout the novel Narayan portrays him under the predominating *Tamas Guna* of lack of self-control. Ramani believes he has done no wrong.

Viswanath in *Grandmother's Tale* is completely under the *Tamas Guna* of **Lack of Self-control.** He is spineless, marries a girl even though he is already married to another. Later, he gets married again to the daughter of his care-taker in a quiet, simple ceremony. He is seventy-five and the girl is seventeen.

In *The World of Nagaraj*, Narayan writes about the man protagonist Nagraj, who is heavily under the dominance of the *Tamas Guna* of **Delusion**:

> ...while he had only been watching and wool-gathering, which were important activities in his scheme of living. Watching and brooding has a subtle value which people never realised. Left to himself he was prepared to sit on the pyol the whole day, looking on the life and movement of Kabir Street (7).

In the novel, *The Financial Expert*, the man protagonist, Margayya is under the *Tamas Guna* of **Ignorance**. He has no value for personal relationships and does not care for his brother. He is 'known to be on throat-cutting terms' (21) with his brother's family. He is intimidated by status and money. He thinks that anyone with power and money has the right to threaten people. He states:

> He has every right because he has more money, authority, dress, looks - above all, more money. It's money which gives people all this. Money alone is important in this world. Everything else will come to us naturally if we have money in our purse (21).

Malgudi is for Narayan the microcosm of India. He writes essentially for *Malgudi* and highlights the fact that human feelings are fundamentally the same. Narayan's memorable characters are all middle class - a class to which he himself belongs. He portrays the tensions, conflicts, finer nuances of human relationships and makes them the basis of his works. His novels highlight interpersonal relationships among parents, children, husband-wife, brother-sister and so on. He depicts men in relationship with other men rather than focusing on man's relationship with God or other abstract things.

Michel Pousse (2012), whose research focusses on 'Narayan as a Gandhian Novelist' states that Narayan has repeatedly stressed the three points which stand out in Gandhi's philosophy.....Life is a never ending quest for truth......Individual peace can only be achieved within a well-defined social context. Village life as opposed to town life is what brings out the best in man (Ed. C.N. Srinath: 61).

M.K. Naik, has offered significant perspectives on Narayan's novels. He points out that Narayan's primary preoccupation is 'with man's fulfilling the life - roles entrusted to him by tradition and environment'. Meenakshi Mukherjee pinpoints Narayan's treatment of the rebellion and comments that the novelist has the belief in Nature's inherent scheme to balance the unruly and disorderly world and to restore peace and order. She states: 'Narayan sees any sudden change not for what new possibilities it brings into existence......but much more negatively as a play of shadows, an illusion, an unreality like a bubble, which will burst open sooner or later and the normal order of the cosmos will prevail again'.

Narayan's writings highlight that empathy and sympathy can make us happy. Many questions get answered in his statement that 'drifting apart is not necessarily an end to our journey with the other. We may meet again in some other form' (*A Tiger for Malgudi*: 176). Narayan's comic mode emphasises that humour can negate several unwanted emotions and heal us. Loss of a dear one followed by conundrums of life get simpler, when we understand that life goes on. No one is indispensable. Finally, even though human relationships are complex, there can be a way to define them. However, evil is self-destructive and one must choose one's thoughts, actions and words carefully.

Researching R.K. Narayan's men protagonists in his fifteen novels, under the influence of *one* out of the *Three Modes of Nature,* gives an insight into our own temperament and personality. These novels then, not only make us conscious of our inherent personality, but paves a path for learning and changing our existing behaviour for the better. Besides, the novels serve to enlighten the higher consciousness and encourage us to move beyond the three *Gunas* 'out of which the body is evolved, to be free from birth, death, decay and pain and attain immortality' (*Bhagvad Gita* : Chapter 14).

Findings of the research can be summarised as follows:

The modes of nature (*Gunas*) are three (*Sattva, Rajas* and *Tamas*). The tendency towards 'purity' comes from *Sattva Guna.* The instinct of 'activity' comes from *Rajas Guna*. The penchant for 'inertia' comes from *Tamas Guna.* The three modes of nature co-exist with each other. However, the predominance of one *Guna* over the other two, shapes a person's personality. This predominating *Guna* is the propelling cause of a person's action and his response towards situations. The impact of the predominating *Guna* also expresses itself in external activities viz. faith, food and charity and internal aspects viz. knowledge, intelligence and will-power.

Researching the men protagonists in R.K. Narayan's novels under the impact of a particular highlighting *Guna* adds a new demission to his writings. The brilliance of Narayan's craftsmanship can be ascertained by the fact that even though he writes of middle-class men in average circumstances living in the fictional town of *Malgudi*, one highlighting *Guna* over the other two *Gunas* can be traced in the personality of each man protagonist throughout the course of the respective novel. For example, in the novel, *The Bachelor of Arts,* the man protagonist talks about 'money'. His personality is under *Rajas Guna* of passion and activity. Margayya, the man protagonist in *The Financial Expert,* on the other hand, talks of 'money' but his disposition is under the influence of *Tamas Guna* of delusion and ignorance. Similarly in the novel *Mr. Sampath,* the man protagonist, while answering the question 'Who are you?' is under the influence of *Rajas Guna* of activity, but The Master in *A Tiger for Malgudi* is under the predominating *Sattva Guna* of wisdom and spirituality when he answers the same question.

Rajas Guna gives rise to desire, ***Tamas Guna*** paves way for inertia and ***Sattva Guna*** brings about wisdom. Reading Narayan's novels and looking at the men protagonists in the new light of a dominating *Guna* fills the lacuna related to his works. This aids in self-discovery and also helps in understanding our *response* which is being governed by a predominating *Guna.* The awareness empowers change in one's personality and attitudes. Most importantly, it helps to attain a non-judgmental view of the other, and makes life happy and simple.

Bibliography

Primary Sources

A. Novels

Narayan, R. K., *Swami and Friends,* London: Hamish Hamilton, 1935; Chicago: University of Chicago Press, 1980.

————, *Bachelor of Arts,* Great Britain: Thomas Nelson and Sons Ltd., 1937; Chicago: University of Chicago Press, 1980.

————, *The Dark Room,* Great Britain: Macmillan and Co., 1938: London: Heinemann, 1978.

————, *The English Teacher,* Great Britain: Eyre and Spottiswoode, 1946 : Chicago University of Chicago Press, 1980.

————, *Mr. Sampath*, London: Eyre and Spottiswoode, 1949: London: Heinemann, 1979.

————, *The Financial Expert*, Great Britain: Methuen and Co. Ltd., 1952.

————, *Waiting for the Mahatma*, London: Methuen and Co. Ltd., 1955.rpt. 2011.

————, *The Guide*, London: Methuen, 1958; Harmondsworth: Penguin, 1980.

————, *The Man-Eater of Malgudi,* London: Wlliam Heinemann Ltd., 1961: Harmonds-worth : Penguin, 1983.

————, *The Vendor of Sweets*, Chennai: Indian Thought Pub., 1967. rpt. 2012.

————, *The Painter of Signs*, London: William Heinemann Ltd., 1977. rpt. 2011.

————, *Talkative Man,* Chennai: Indian Thought Pub., 1983. rpt. 2011.

————, *A Tiger for Malgudi*, Chennai: Indian Thought Pub., 1986. rpt 2009

————, *The World of Nagaraj*, London: Heinemann, 1990.

————, *The Grandmother's Tale*, Mysore: Indian Thought Pub., 1992. rpt 2011.

Secondary Sources:

Anand, Mulk Raj, *Untouchable*, New Delhi : An Orient Paperback, 1970.

————, *Apology for Heroism,* New Bombay: Kutub Popular,1957.

Arya, R.N., 'Characterisation in the Malgudi: Novels of R.K. Narayan' in *Critical Response to RK Narayan*, Ed. Prasad, New Delhi: A.N. Sarup and Sons, 2003.

Baghmar, G. P., *R.K. Narayan*, Nagpur: Vishwa Bharti Prakashan, 1992.

Biswal, Jayant K., *A Critical Study of the Novels of R.K. Narayan*, New Delhi: Nirmal, 1987.

Biswal, S.K., *R. K. Narayan: A Critical Study*, Delhi: Omega Publications, 2011.

Biswas, Sarwani, *A Study of RK Narayan's Novels - A celebration of the Carnival,* New Delhi: Atlantic 2010.

Chapple, C.K., *Non-Violence to Animals, Earth and Self in Asian Traditions,* U.S.A.: State University of New York Press, 1993.

Derette, M.E., *The Modern Indian Novel in English,* Brussels: English 'Universite' Libre, 1966.

Dewari, D.S., Gandhian Bearings on R.K. Narayan's Novels, New Delhi: Atlantic, 2010.

————, *The Use of Myth in R.K. Narayan's Novels*, New Delhi: Prestige, 2001.

Dnyate, Ramesh. *The Novels of R.K. Narayan: a Typological Study of Characters,* New Delhi: Prestige, 2000.

Dominic, K.V., Multicultural Consciousness in the novels of R.K. Narayan, Delhi: Authorpress, 2012.

Dubey, Meenu, *Myths, Legends and Reality in the novels of Mulk Raj Anand, R.K. Narayan and Raja Rao*, New Delhi; Swaroop Book Publishers, 2010.

Forster, E.M., Preface to *Untouchable,* A Novel by Mulk Raj Anand, New Delhi: Orient Paperback, 1970.

Gor, Uday C., *The Child in R.K. Narayan's Fiction. A study,* Jaipur: Mark Publication, 2011.

Greene, Graham, *Introduction to The Bachelor of Arts and the Financial Expert,* Mysore: Indian Thought Publication, 1977.

————, *Introduction. The Financial Expert By R.K. Narayan,* Mysore: Indian Thought Publication, 1977.

Holmstrom Lakshmi, *The Novels of R. K. Narayan*, Calcutta: The Writers' Workshop, 1973.

Iyengar, K.R., *Indian Writing in English*, New Delhi: Sterling, 1985.

Joshi, Prakash M., *Artistic and Realistic Mode in R.K. Narayan's Fiction*, Jaipur: Aadi Publication, 2014.

Kundu, AK., *Vedanta and Myth: A Study of RK Narayan's Novel,* Jaipur: Book Enclave, 2009.

Madhukar, Nikam, *Colonial and Post Colonial identity in R.K. Narayan's Novels,* Nagpur: Dattsons, 2013.

Naik, M. K., *The Ironic Vision: A Study of the Fiction of R.K. Narayan*, New Delhi: Sterling Publishers, 1983.

————, *A History of Indian English Literature*. New Delhi: Sahitya Akademi Publications, 1999.

Naik, M.K., S.K. Desai and G.S. Amur (eds), *Critical Essays on Indian Writing in English,* Dharwar, 1976.

Narayanan, R., *Psyche- Moral Comic sense in R.K. Narayan's Novels,* Germany: LAP Lambert Academy Publishing, 2012.

Oxford Dictionary Thesaurus & Wordpower Guide, 35th ed. London Oxford University Press, 2006.

Pattanaik, Devdutt, *My Gita*, New Delhi: Rupa Publication, 2015.

Pattanayak, Nityananda, *R.K. Narayan A Study in Narrative Technique*, New Delhi: Adhyayan Publishers and Distributers, 2012.

Pousse, Michel, *R. K. Narayan: A Painter of Modern India*, New York: Peter Lang, 1995.

Putatunda, Sarbani (ed.), *R.K. Narayan Critical Essays*, New Delhi: PHI, Learning Private Ltd., 2012.

Qazi, Khursheed Ahmad, *A Lacanian Reading of R.K. Narayan's Novels,* New Delhi: Alfa Publication, 2012.

Rizwan, Md. S., *The Existence of Life in Novel's of R.K. Narayan,* Germany: LAP Lambert Academy Publishing, 2012.

Ram, Susan and Ram, N., *R.K. Narayan: The Early Years: 1906-1945,* New Delhi: Viking, 1996.

Ramteke, S.R., *R.K. Narayan and his Social Perspectives*, New Delhi: Atlantic, 1998.

Rao, Ranga, *R.K. Narayan*, New Delhi: Sahitya Akademi, 2004.

Sen, Krishna, *Critical Essays on R.K. Narayan's The Guide: With an Introduction to Narayan's Novels*, Kolkata: Orient Longman, 2004.

Singh, P.K., *The Novels of R.K. Narayan : A Critical Evolution*, New Delhi : Atlantic Publishers and Distributors, 2014.

Srinath, C.N., *R.K. Narayan: An Anthology of Recent Criticism*, New Delhi: Pencraft International, 2005.

The Bhagvad Gita, Swami Childhavanand (trans.), Tirupparaintturai: Sri Ram Krishna Tapovana, 1975, 8th impression.

Thieme, John, *R.K. Narayan Contemporary World Writers,* U.K.: Manchester University Press, 2007.

———, *RK Narayan*. New Delhi: Viva Books, 2010.

Tripathi, Dhananjay, *R.K. Narayan: Phenomenology and Consciousness*, Germany: Scholars' Press, 2012.

Walsh, William, *R. K. Narayan: A Critical Appreciation*, Great Britain: University of Chicago Press, 1982.

Articles

Atkinson, D. W., 'Spiritual Growth in the Fiction of R.K. Narayan', *Asian Profile,* 13 (3), 1985.

Gaur, K. K., 'Women in R. K. Narayan's Early Novels', in Amarnath Prasad (ed.), *Critical Response to R. K. Narayan*, New Delhi: Sarup and Sons, 2003: 171-218.

Kaul, A.N., 'R.K. Narayan and the East West Theme', *Considerations,* Meenakshi Mukherjee (ed.), New Delhi: Allied, 1977.

Kohli, Suresh, 'Views on Indian Novelists: An Interview with R.K. Narayan', *Indian and Foreign Review*, 7, 1975: 13-20.

Kothandaraman, Bala, 'The Time Dimension in R. K. Narayan's Novels', *Journal of South Asian Literature*, 22 (2), 1987: 28-33.

Lever, Susan, 'The Comedy of Misreading in the Fiction of R.K. Narayan', *R.K. Narayan: Critical Perspectives*, A.L. McLeod (ed.), New Delhi: Sterling, 1994: 76-85.

Naik, M.K., 'Theme and Form in R.K. Narayan's The Man-Eater of Malgudi', *Journal of Commonwealth Literature,* 10(3), 1976.

Nair, Rama, 'Gunas as Determinants of Character: A study of R.K. Narayan's The Guide', *Osmania Journal of English Studies* 26, 1990: 41-48.

Narayan, R.K., 'Self-Obituary No.5', *Illustrated Weekly of India*, 23 July 1950.

Pousse, Michel, 'Narayan as a Gandhian Novelist', *The Journal of Indian Writing in English*, 19 (2), July 1991.

Ram, N. & Susan Ram, 'Narayan of Malgudi: Sixty-Five Years of Story- Telling', *Frontline*, 13(20), 18 October 1996.

Ram, N., 'R.K. Narayan in The First Person', *Frontline,* 27, 2010.

Raman, Ashalata, 'Depiction of Childhood in R. K. Narayan's Novels', *Mahmul,* 1 (1), 2011: 53-59.

Rao, K. B. Ramakrishna, 'The Gunas of Prakriti according to the Samkhya Philosophy', *Philosophy East and West*, 13 (1), April 1963: 61-71.

Rao, Ranga, 'Narayan's Unique Comedy', *The Hindu*, 7 October 2001.

Sihra, Karen, 'Philosophical Contribution of Gandhi's ideas on Non- Violence', Research and practice in Social Sciences 2 (1), 2006: 40-52.

Srinath, C. N., 'R. K. Narayan's Comic Vision: Possibilities and Limitations', *World Literature Today*, 55 (3), 1981: 416-19.

Tiwary, Shyam Bihari, 'Old Wine in New Bottles: Traditionalism in R.K. Narayan's Novels', *Cyber Literature* 15-16 (1-2), 2005: 14-28.

Web Publications

Commonwealth Novelists: R.K. Narayan and V.S. Naipaul, "The Sewanee Review, 21 Oct. 2010. www.jostor.org

Garbebian, Keith. "Strategy and Theme in the Art of R.K. Narayan," Ariel: A Review of International English Literature, 5.4 (1974): 70-8.7 July, 2011.www.ariel.synergiesprairies.

https://enwikipedia.google.oo.in>books https://enwikipedia.

org>wiki.Platonic epistemology https://enwikipedia.

Org.wiki>ignorance

ir in flibnet.ac.in>jspui>bitstream

Kothandaraman, Bala, "The Time Dimension in R.K. Narayan's Novels," Journal of South Asian Literature, 22.2 (1987): 28.33. 13 July, 2011 www.jstor.org

Mukherjee, Meenakshi, "The Anxiety of Indianness: Our Novels in English," Economics and Political Weekly, 28,48 (1993): 2607-2611. 21 Nov. 2009, www.jstor.org

Narayan, R.K., 21 Aug. 2010 en.wikipedia.org

Poulet, George, "Phenomenology of Reading" 23 Oct, 2011. www.jstor.org

Rao, Ranga, 14 June, 2011 www.outloook.india.com

Riemenschneider, Dieter. "The Train Has Moved on" R.K. Narayan's The Guide and Literary History. Asiatic, Vol. 3 No. 2 Dec. 2009.

11 June, 2011 ww.asiantic.iium.edu.my

Index

P

R

S